A PLACE TO GO ON FROM

A PLACE TO GO ON FROM

The Collected Poems of

Iain Lonie

~

Edited by
David Howard

Published by Otago University Press
PO Box 56 / Level 1, 398 Cumberland Street
Dunedin, New Zealand
university.press@otago.ac.nz
www.otago.ac.nz/press

First published 2015
Copyright © David Howard, The Estate of Bill Sewell, Damian Love
(as named)
and The Estate of Iain Lonie, 2015
Volume copyright © Otago University Press
ISBN 978-1-927322-01-7

A catalogue record for this book is available from the National Library
of New Zealand. This book is copyright. Except for the purpose of
fair review, no part may be stored or transmitted in any form or by any
means, electronic or mechanical, including recording or storage in any
information retrieval system, without permission in writing from the
publishers. No reproduction may be made, whether by photocopying or
by any other means, unless a licence has been obtained from the publisher.

Cover image: *The Centurion's Servant* (1914), Stanley Spencer (1891–
1959), oil on canvas, © Tate, London

Publisher: Rachel Scott
Editor: Damian Love
Design & typesetting: Damian Love

Printed in China through Asia Pacific Offset Ltd

Contents

Preface 17
Acknowledgements 20
Chronology · Bridie Lonie 21
Iain Lonie: A Memoir · Bill Sewell 25
Dead Reckoning: The Poetry of Iain Lonie · Damian Love 31

I DIGGING TO THE ANTIPODES

'Rubbing my hand along the rough-cast wall' 57
'Now spring dawns in our months of passion' 57
'The fisherman's line startled' 58
Solstice 58
Allardyce 59
Fragment 59
Holiday Notes
   1 Evening 60
   2 Morning 60
   3 Night Passage 60
Tarawera 61
'Why will you stand so, against the winter sky' 62
Song 62
By a River 63
Sonnet 63
Scottish Mill Towns 64
'Give to all youth this I have known' 64

'At whoring I was ineffectual' 65
Letter from a Distance 65
Wickliffe Bay
   The Sea Fog 66
   The Hay Field 67
   Morning Calm 68
Letter from a Ferry 69
Idiot's Song 71
from Remarks on a Landscape Painting 73
The Real McCoy 73
Lifer 74
Witch 75
from 'The rose-tree in my garden grew suddenly still' 75
The Achaeans 76
Elegy, Armidale Cemetery 78
'Perhaps it is its death' 80
Dialogue 81
'Once again I recognise that coast black as iron' 82
'Having taken that decision, you could not see' 83
from 'As the grey river brought me round again' 84
The Forced Listener 84
from The Wind at Rimini
   1 Her Room 86
   2 Her Dreams 87
   3 Cosi vidi venir, traendo guai, ombre portate dalla detta briga 87
   4 Last Night 88
   5 'I drove past your house last night' 89
Elegy to Maecenas 90
Kallimachos of Kyrene 91
Request for a Birthday Poem 92
'No fog: merely a thickening of air' 93

'Adjectives—something thrown in for good measure' 93
From a Point of View 94
Matutinal 95
At Pearl Bay 96
Cunning Odysseus 97

II RECREATIONS (1967, 1970)

Part One

1 'Shop windows turn their light upon the street' 101
2 'It may happen at any time, for any cause: your pen' 101
3 'On the sand hill, lupin blooms' 102
4 'The dress you wear' 103
5 'Some women, they say, in your circumstances' 103
6 Orpheus to Eurydice 104
7 'Now he has gone, in petulance or boredom' 104
8 'When the act we would' 105
9 'Between the time of you and I' 105

Part Two

10 'One may grow angry with it: it is like a person' 106
11 'All that night, and through the next and through the next' 107
12 'Still ignorant of his power, he essayed' 107
13 'This man perished beyond the speed of sound' 108
14 'Not the breath of the rabble, acrid with lust now' 108
15 Electra 109
16 'Their forefathers, moving through a fluent' 110
17 Death 110

Part Three

   18 'To hide one's madness among the mad' 111
   19 'The worst part is the waking dream' 111
   20 'Leaves fall, leaves fall' 112
   21 'She is young, young as the green grape' 113
   22 'Lift your head, stag, lift your antlered head' 113
   23 'After years, he learned to welcome the summer' 114
   24 'In the spring and autumn, mice invade my house' 114
   25 'The children across the road were undesirable' 115
   26 'Grace in this landscape is hard to find' 116
   27 'We who never cared for gardens' 117

III LIVING FOR OTHERS

'The snow melts quickly from the hills' 121
'I do not claim' 121
from 'I think of you' 122
'Why do you put up with me?' 122
'If in the morning' 124
Traditio 125
Glacier 125
Short Story 127
'We return from a walk together' 129
The Green Bird 131
'You died at nineteen' 132
'Unaccompanied by dog or memory' 133
Dee Why Morning 134
Epitaph 135
Erinna's Lament for Baukis 135
Ugolino and His Sons 137
Nothing to Do with Us 139

Dunedin Weather 139
Two Houses 140

IV LETTERS FROM EPHESUS (1970)

From Academy Hill 143
Street Scene 144
Four Sydney Photographs 145
Academic Architecture 147
Letter from Ephesus 148
Studies 152

V SEEING THE ISLAND

Afternoon Tea in the East 157
Ode to Walter 158
West Berlin: Unorchestrated Notes 158
Memories of Ithaca 160
Country Walk with Guide-book 163
Change of Season on the Way to the Station 164
'A canteen is provided' 165
Death of a Culture 166
'In washing dishes, she sought her usual end' 167
Territorial Dispute 168
Now We Are 168
Home Thoughts from Abroad 169
Pioneers 170
'I am a small boy' 171
'A beautiful dark haired girl runs' 171
A Dull Man, Essentially 172
Your Story 173

Jazz Record Requests 173
A Summer Night 174
'Whitley Rocks' 175
Friends at the Funeral 176
Winter Strawberries 176
Third Party 177
Saying and Meaning 177
Homoeoteleuton 178

VI COURTING DEATH (1984)

'Why, when I speak, do you never answer?' 183
Anomalous Behaviour 183
Point of No Return 184
By Foreign Hands 184
Five o'clock 185
Creatures of the Fire 186
Ghosts 186
Tonight 192
Cupboard Love 192
Travel Diary 193
A Postcard of Cornwall 193
On the Equator 194

VII THE CLASSIC CAST OF GRIEF

Purakanui Birdcall 197
The Divide 198
Truth 199

Interviews of Eyes 199
Lifelike 200
Death Porno 201
'and in that way' 202
Talent 205
Dual Number 205
Bricolage
   1 Green Bottle 206
   2 Cardboard Box 206
   3 Cut Glass I 207
   4 Cut Glass II 208
   5 Wrack 208
   6 Cranach: Adam and Eve 209
   7 Dolce Vita 209
Things No Longer Simple 210
Second Chance 210
Lines on a Photograph 211
from 3½ Poems About the Weather for R.
   1 I'm glad you rang 212
   2 I like you a lot 213
   3½ Can we meet again sometime? 214
Here is My Song for Death: Lydian Chant 214
The First of March 215
'But' 216
Conversation 217
'The evenings are hot' 218
The Blankness of Snow 219
Haunted House 220
The House of Childhood 220
Waikanae, with Vanessa and Toby 221

VIII THE ENTRANCE TO PURGATORY (1986)

Part One

Flying Back
  1 Rome 1965 225
  2 Pieces of Occasion 225
  3 Flying Back 226
Dead Letter 227
Choices 228
Your Old Age 229
The Frog Prince 230
Vacuum Flask 230
Your Dream 231
Visit 231
The World Outside 232
Night Garden, with Ghost 234
Im wunderschönen Monat Mai 234
Autumn Thunder 236
Two Nocturnes
  1 Dispossession: staccato 237
  2 Possession: legato 238
Old Friends 239
Ending the Sentence 240

Part Two

Crusoe's Canoe 241
We Are All in a Painting 244
Horace's Girlfriends 245
Theory of the Leisure Class, 1983 246
A Flat in WC1 246
Fine Definitions 247

Among the Ruins
   1 In Padua 248
   2 Loch Ewe 250
   3 Val di Chiana 250
   4 Sydney 251
   5 A Country Hard to Imagine 252
   6 In the Third Person 253
An Oblique View 255
The Compass Points North 258
The Entrance to Purgatory 260

IX THE HEART'S HARD EDGE

A Late Honeymoon
   1 Voiles 265
   2 Nuages 266
   3 Brouillards 266
Voices 267
Slow Glass 268
Tarawera, Lake & Mountain 269
Journey North 269
'Dear Ann, this present I enclose' 275
Not a Poem 276
Le Grand Meaulnes 277
Watching War Films 278
By Definition 279
Letter in December 279
Reflets dans l'eau 281
At Least 282

X WINTER WALK AT MORNING (1991)

Odysseus in Travelland 285
Philemon and Baucis 286
Dead Reckoning 286
Cambridge in the Fifties
   1 *11.30 from Liverpool Street* 288
   2 *In the Mill Lane Lecture Rooms* 289
Lines on a Photograph 290
Exile 291
Ancestral Ground 292
Folk Memory 294
Mirror Language 295
A Summer at Purakanui 296
Caliban at the Typewriter 297
Waking Up in Naples 299
Nearly So 301
Distances 303
Holy Loch 304
Two Predicates 306
My Toaster Tells the Time 307
April the First 308
The Art of Poetry 309
Knowing the Right Places 309
The Winter Walk at Morning 311
From the Heartland 313
Unattended Crossing Ahead 314
Harriet Martineau: First Intimations of Politics and
      Death 315
Variation on an Old Theme 316
Collection Day 318

Proposal at Allans Beach 319
Mind Your Head 321
Hanging the Washing Out 321

XI BEING OUTSIDE TIME: versions from Eugenio Montale (1985–87)

Letter from the Riviera di Levante 327
'Since life escapes us' 331
'Good Linuccia, you who climb' 332
Jovian 332
My Friend Péa 333
Oboe 334
Monologue 334
'How the horizon narrows' 335
Hiding Places 336
A Visitor 337
Succulents 338
Within/Without 339
'My Swiss watch was faulty' 340
'To me it's just impossible' 340
'Wipe your glasses if they are dimmed' 341
A Pupil of the Muses 341
Daybreak 342
The Coastguard's House 343

Sources 345
Notes 347
Index of titles 379
Index of first lines 383

Preface

As early as 1954 Iain Lonie observed: 'Poetry is a sort of conjuring trick … we would like to know how the poet abstracts the pigeon from our jacket, of whose existence we were unaware' [MS-3619/033]. The business of becoming a poet necessarily becomes a meditation on being. After the heroes of Homer came the anti-hero of Archilochus. In his memoir Bill Sewell describes Lonie as 'wounded'. One of the men who presents in Lonie's letters, journals and diaries is witty, considerate and loving; another is worried, uncertain of his worth, even peevish. They both belong to the poetry, which is personal if not always personable. Often, alongside irony, there is the saving grace of compassion. It is this compassion that calls the mature poetry to account, that is the measure of its quality.

'To express: to press or voyage out' [MS-2674/143]. A survey of the chronology provided by Lonie's eldest daughter, Bridie, confirms that Lonie had a peripatetic, tempestuous, yet meditative life. Whether as a starred first scholar from Cambridge or a star-struck poet who was not so much displaced as unplaced, he was always preparing to go; it became a vocation, one confirmed by the sudden death of his second wife, Judith. From her absence, an absence that accompanied him wherever he went, he made poetry that wandered through the quotidian yet also leapt towards if not altogether into the ineffable. But Lonie explored the archetypal Judith's absence *before* he lost her, as a reading of these creepily prescient lines from 'The Wind at Rimini' shows:

> It was as though someone had closed your staring eyes
> Not out of pity, but with a desire for tidiness
> And had gone away then, swinging the keys.

It is a truism that we find what we are looking for—Lonie believed that we largely make our own tragedies—however, he was forced by what he termed Judith's 'annihilation' to decently bury then indecently resurrect her in words. As Damian Love avers in his essay, 'Love gets into things.' But to redeem the muse is to justify the maker. Lonie's mature work is more than remembrance. If it is a set of spells to summon the physically dead, then it is also an attempt to recover the loved in himself. There is intimate detail yet it is too easy to treat that poetry as bareback confessional; its urgency is worked for, even learned. Suspicious of what he called the 'rhetoric of grief', the poet was still instructed by the scholar who acknowledged that: 'A theory which is internally consistent may not be true—may not, in Plato's terms, yield *episteme*—but it is at least clear or intelligible: it is a *saphes logos*. Now in Greek a *saphes logos*, such as for example might be brought by a messenger in a tragedy, is one in which "everything fits together" in such a way as to create a presumption of its truth' ['De natura pueri, ch. 13']. In Lonie's own poetry particulars are arranged to advance an informing narrative that compels. Each late poem is a *saphes logos*. And we can hear the echo in 'Crusoe's Canoe': 'they'll hold themselves together for you'.

But it takes time. To adapt an analogy from Montaigne, in the considered business that was Lonie's early work the real dealing, where head and heart are held to account by language, seems to take place in a closed private room behind the store signposted POETRY. The pieces he chose to publish are less striking than those he left on the shelf. This may help explain why he was undervalued. If 'Elegy to Maecenas', 'Short Story' and 'Ugolino and His Sons' had been known by the close of the 1960s then readers might have visited regularly rather than passing by. But in Lonie's mature work the private room opens onto the street. When he eavesdrops on his grief he lets us read our own dislocation (loss is always dislocating) into the most poised body of elegiac poetry New Zealand has. Because consciousness is porous we realise that, after Judith's death, this private room with its open door is Lonie's version of conviviality, a conviviality that extends back through Montale to Dante yet dazzlingly anticipates the domestic focus of younger New Zealand poets. Now we can say hello, knowing that Iain Lonie's poetry is 'a place to go on from'.

David Howard
Dunedin, January 2015

Acknowledgements

I am grateful to the Lonie family, principally Andrew, Bridie, David, Jonathan and Sally, for their warming confidence; to Ann Somerville for surrendering the letters and poems sent to her by Iain Lonie; to the staff of the Hocken Collections for their congenial professionalism as I excavated unpublished poems and cross-referenced notebooks, diaries and letters; to Alan Roddick for permission to quote from the papers of Charles Brasch; to Peter Simpson for drawing my attention to entries about Lonie in Brasch's unpublished journals; to Thomas Forster for his close reading of the early material collected in the first section 'Digging to the Antipodes'; to Maurice Andrew for identifying a letter in the *BBC Listener* dated 14 October 1954; to Paola Voci for her support as I stumbled through Lonie's Italian influences, Dante and Montale; to Damian Love for his introductory essay; to Harry Ricketts for his help in contacting Amanda Powell, and to Amanda for permission to publish the memoir by Bill Sewell; to Cilla McQueen, Bill Manhire and Vincent O'Sullivan for their thoughts. The final push on this project was provided by the appointment of the editor to the Robert Burns Fellowship 2013 by the University of Otago; to the staff in the Department of English and Linguistics, a bow.

Chronology

༄

1932	Born to Thomas Christie Lonie and Edith Hephzibah Lonie (née Smith) in March, Cambridgeshire. T. C. Lonie was County Medical Officer of Health in the Isle of Ely. An elder brother, Thomas Christie Macbeth Lonie, was born in Malaysia in 1928.
1936	Younger brother David Alistair born.
1938	Moves to Glasgow where T. C. Lonie is in general practice.
1942	Emigrates to New Zealand, residing at Gisborne, where T. C. Lonie is Medical Officer of Health.
1945	Applies for entry to Dartmouth Naval Academy but is rejected because of being colour-blind.
1946	Moves to Palmerston North.
1948	Friendship with the Garland family in Wellington. First nervous breakdown.
1949	Commences studies at Otago University. Initially enrolled in English, he transfers to Classics in 1950.
1951	Marries science student Jean Stella Andrews (1930–1997), whom he had met in the Carrington Hall of Residence. Daughter Bridie born.
1952	Moves to Wickliffe Bay (in Papanui Inlet), then to Pukehiki, both on the Otago Peninsula, commuting to university by motorcycle. Developing friendship with Charles Brasch.

1953   Son Jonathan born.

1954   Commences the Classical tripos at King's College, Cambridge University.

1956   Second nervous breakdown. Son Angus born. Visits Italy with Jean. Gains starred first in Ancient Philosophy. Accepts a position in Classics at the University of New England, Armidale, New South Wales.

1957–59 Teaches at the University of New England. Produces Bernard Shaw's *Arms and the Man* and acts in Chekhov's *The Cherry Orchard*.

1960   Accepts position at the University of Sydney.

1961   Meets Judith Black (née Benson, b. 1937), a postgraduate student in his department.

1962   Daughter Alison (Sally) born. In November leaves for sabbatical in Cambridge. First visit to Greece, followed by a stay in Rome.

1963   Begins working on the history of medicine. Travels in Cornwall and Scotland. Publishes, with C.K. Stead, a translation of Euripides' *Alcestis*, in *Mask and Microphone: Six Plays*, selected and edited by Leslie Rees (Angus & Robertson).

1964   In March returns to Sydney. Resigns from University of Sydney and accepts position at University of Otago.

1965   In January moves to Dunedin.

1966   In the New Year leaves his wife Jean for Judith Black, who moves to Dunedin with her daughter Jennifer (b. 1957).

1967   *Recreations* published.

1967–69 Acts at the Globe Theatre in Dunedin, including a performance as the Cardinal in *The Duchess of Malfi*.

1969   Marries Judith Black.

1970	*Letters from Ephesus* published. Judith Lonie (Benson) self-publishes chapbook *Seascapes*.
1971	Sabbatical in London and Berlin to work on edition of Hippocratic texts with Dr Gerhard Baader. Travels to Italy (twice) and to Greece. Judith Lonie publishes *Earth into Moon* (Bibliography Room, University of Otago, Dunedin).
1972	Returns to Classics Department at Otago.
1973	Son Andrew born.
1974	Resigns from Classics Department; commences work on Harbour Board dredge (where he often cleans the bilges, 'Dante's punishment for the gluttonous'). Gains nautical qualification at night school.
1976	In September presents paper at Mons Colloquium on Hippocratic texts. Gains Wellcome Institute Fellowship in London for further work on Hippocratic texts.
1977	Commences study at Wellington's Library School, but returns to Dunedin in April. Commences work at Otago Catchment Board as researcher and librarian.
1978	Judith gains entry to Newcastle University's speech therapy degree programme. In September Iain, Judith and Andrew move to Jesmond, Newcastle. Gains four-year fellowship at Wellcome Institute. During the fellowship goes twice to Italy and travels frequently through northern England and Scotland.
1981	Publishes *The Hippocratic Treatises, 'On Generation', 'On the Nature of the Child', 'Diseases IV': A Commentary* (Berlin and New York: Walter de Gruyter).
1982	In August completes Wellcome Institute scholarship; Judith, her studies completed, gains a position at

	Newcastle Hospital as a speech therapist. On 18 December she dies of an aortic aneurism (initially diagnosed as a cerebral haemorrhage).
1983	In April returns to Dunedin with Andrew. Works at the Otago Catchment Board as a librarian.
1984	Assistant editor at John McIndoe Press, working with Brian Turner and Bill Sewell. *Courting Death* published.
1985	Edits, with A. Wear and R.K. French, *The Medical Renaissance of the Sixteenth Century* (Cambridge University Press), contributing 'The Paris Hippocratics: Teaching and research in Paris in the second half of the sixteenth century'.
	Edits Judith Lonie's *The Remembering of the Elements* (John McIndoe).
	Starts corresponding with Ann Somerville; they first meet in person during the New Year holiday in 1986.
1986	*The Entrance to Purgatory* published.
1987	Editor at the University of Otago Press.
1988	On 18 June, on the season-appropriate anniversary of Judith's death, in increasing distress and fearful that he might suffer the mental illness of his youth, takes his own life.
1991	*Winter Walk at Morning* published.

Bridie Lonie
Dunedin, January 2015

Iain Lonie: A Memoir
Bill Sewell

I always thought of Iain Lonie as a 'wounded' person. It is true that I knew him for less than five years, having met him not twelve months after the sudden death of his wife Judith. But I always sensed that the 'wound' was more fundamental than simple grief—not that grief is simple—that it was cut out of the man's extraordinary sensibility. I believe that he just felt everything too deeply.

On hearing of Iain's death by his own hand, I experienced a number of reactions. An unnatural calm, to begin with; then a feeling of companionship which persisted for most of the rest of the day, as I read his letters and poems, talked with him in my mind: anger, of course, that he had deprived me of his friendship; and finally, panic, a blast of the cosmic wind. But amongst all this, I found the words of Kent at the end of *King Lear* running through my head:

> Vex not his ghost: O! let him pass; he hates him
> That would upon the rack of this tough world
> Stretch him out longer.

I was greatly saddened by Iain's death; but I felt no particular surprise, and, for him, even a sense of relief.

Though I was living in Dunedin as early as 1974 I didn't actually meet Iain until nearly a decade later. By that time, of course, he had long since abandoned—on a point of principle, I understand—the secure (and senior) academic position he had earned as the outstanding scholar he was, and was employed in one of the series of short-term jobs he held subsequently. I was a PEP worker, supposed to be sorting out the 'archives' of the Silverpeaks County Council, but in my solitude was writing a lot of poetry. One day, towards the end of 1983, Iain was introduced to me as the temporary librarian—a position more exalted than mine, though I suspect no more appreciated. There was an instant rapport, and mutual respect: he knew something of my work, I something of his reputation. Before long, while our fellow workers talked at afternoon tea about gardening and football and septic tanks, Iain and I talked poetry.

Physically, the man was an enigma. So thin and hollow-chested he looked malnourished; yet he was an energetic cyclist, accompanying his son Andrew on long rides to the peninsula, and also, by all accounts, an intrepid yachtsman. A face lined enough to betray his years, and a skeletal set of teeth; and yet blond hair that never—though I didn't inspect closely—had a strand of grey in it. He was aging, yet ageless. There was also something of the clown about him: a large red nose, which you might have taken for a drinker's nose, except that Iain's hangovers were too vicious to allow him that kind of solace. And his mode of dress: I could never decide whether it was deliberately somewhat bohemian—a little too colourful, yet lacking in colour coordination—or whether he had no dress sense (I recently discovered that he was colour-blind). But always, for work, he wore a tie; and this seemed to place him a generation or two ahead of mine.

If he was a clown, then it was only the sad clown he represented, whose aim was to wring laughter from life's absurdities and injustices. His poems—which will be his real legacy, after all our memories have evaporated—are not glib, one-dimensional, crowd-pleasing performance-pieces. The very best of them are about death—he even entitled one of his collections *Courting Death*—and how to cope with it, to stare it out. In the end, of course, he was the one to blink.

It is too early for me to give an objective appraisal of Iain Lonie's poems. But I can say now that his great achievement was that even when writing out of his agony, he was able to remain detached, giving his poems a measured and cool, though no less intense, character. This short piece, 'Your Old Age', Hardyesque in its simplicity and poignancy, illustrates what I mean:

> A slight accident
> a bandaged leg
> and a walking stick
> a theatrical prop
> to amuse us all
> still did not stop
> your walk in the wood:
> the bluebells
> as you passed
> drew back in comment
> upon an invisible wind
> then nodded forward to stillness.
>
> So brief your old age:
> a project considered
> and quietly rejected.

I remember Iain once telling me that, yes, the process of grieving was insufferable, but it was also immensely *interesting*. Out of this interest came the ability to observe, note, make magnificent poetry.

During much of the time I knew Iain he was working through this phase of grief poetically, and sometimes despaired that he would ever have anything else to write about. He was boring even *himself* with the subject, he said. Perhaps himself, but not his friends and admirers. I had the privilege to edit his last—and to date, finest—volume, *The Entrance To Purgatory* (John McIndoe, 1986). In his humility, he could sometimes be a maddening author to work with: indecisive about which poems to include, and which to omit, and too willing to leave himself in his editor's hands. In the end we managed to fashion a collection with a compelling argument to it: beginning with grief, and in the second part moving beyond it into what I hoped was to be a phase of reconstruction. 'Crusoe's Canoe', the poem in four sections which opens the second part, hints at this: 'You have to let things die / in their own gentle way // to sail off from the island.' And then there's the title poem, my favourite of all Iain's poems, with its classical balance of rhetoric and restraint. It belongs in that great tradition of 'Dunedin poems', moulded by Bracken, Brasch, Baxter, Tuwhare, Ruth Dallas, Brian Turner, Cilla McQueen and many others. Its theme—and its triumph—is the reconciliation of the Old and the New Worlds, and the poet's determination to rebuild his life somehow:

> Later you must unpack
> pictures and broken ornaments, making them
> the measure of your loss, and what it takes to forgive.
> Here too the city will help, hill tree and tower
> by sunlight or by starlight assembled into a setting
> for something to take place in, a place to go on from.

But it must not be forgotten, amongst all the pain, that Iain had enormous affability and wit. Not only could he be a most entertaining dinner-guest, he allowed his sense of humour to enter his poems. One example will suffice. Iain suffered dreadfully from writer's block, that periodic inability to 'spark' that afflicts all but the most superficial of poets. Then, suddenly, the neurons would begin firing again; and he once encapsulated the exhilaration of this in an ingenious—if perhaps sexist—image in the unpublished sonnet 'Dolce Vita': 'Last night, for me, / the Muse took off her pantyhose and I knew I'd made it.'

During his lifetime Iain was not given his due as a poet in this country. He was never included in the major anthologies—filled as they are with flashier and in the end less enduring lights—and though *The Entrance to Purgatory* was shortlisted for the New Zealand Book Awards in 1987, it has broken no sales records. One can only guess as to why this should be so. Literary success is something of a lottery: it is dependent on fashion, time and place, on image and assertiveness. Iain refused to submit to modish dictates as to what a poem should be (though most of his work was no less rooted in the contemporary); he spent much of his mature writing life outside New Zealand; and he was not one to 'market' his work.

In fact, he could be self-effacing to a fault. I have never known anyone who was able to *listen* so intently as Iain—as if, when you were merely prattling on, for him you were unlocking the secrets of the universe. He and I exchanged work at regular intervals; and while he would dismiss his own offerings on the one hand, he was generous with his praise for mine on the other. But if he felt that I was not writing to my own standards, he was not afraid to say so. Twice he quoted at me a dictum of Peter Porter's (a poet he admired unreservedly): 'Perhaps you should try to say something more interesting than you really mean.' Another time he suggested that I wasn't 'taking enough risks, and that (technically) everything's a bit too tidy'. He was right, of course; and as much as I miss his friendship, I shall miss his gentle and judicious criticism.

I had left Dunedin for Wellington by the time of Iain's final crisis. I knew of it from the last telephone conversation we had—brutally interrupted by someone else on the line wanting something trivial—and also from mutual friends. I suspected that the situation was grave, but restricted my reaction to writing a supportive letter. With a suicide one feels one could have done more; and there is a sense of personal responsibility. I feel this all the more keenly because during a dark period of my life, Iain was unobtrusively kind to me. He made me welcome in his house, listened to my troubles, and at the end of an evening would bring out the bottle of Laphroaig, the malt whisky we both relished, but which made both of us suffer terribly the following day.

Of course, this was merely a transient physical suffering, not the debilitating emotional suffering which dogged him for so long. And now, for Iain, suffering—of whatever kind—is no longer an issue. But he leaves his poems to help us understand his, and indeed our own, suffering.

July 1988

Dead Reckoning: The Poetry of Iain Lonie
Damian Love

There is some measure of distinction, perhaps, in being the foremost poet ignored by one's compatriots. It was never a status he resigned himself to, indeed it rightly troubled him, for despite all diffidence he knew his worth. But Iain Lonie's timing was bad: his five slim volumes spanned a period, from 1967 to 1991, that was not receptive to his voice. He wrote with the precision and passionate restraint of a classical style at a time when avant-garde enthusiasms favoured disjunction, demotic speech and aggressive experiment. He explored a private bereavement, and bereavement's essential privacy, while his fellow poets were hastening to map their race and gender onto the body politic. And he addressed a deracinated culture when fashion had moved on to standing conspicuously upright. His virtues were not those which dominated New Zealand poetry in those decades.

To read him now is, for most of us, practically to discover a new resource. It is easy to imagine someone chancing upon him for the first time, without prejudice or expectation, or nearly so, and turning casually to a poem like 'Your Old Age':

> A slight accident
> a bandaged leg
> and a walking stick
> a theatrical prop
> to amuse us all
> still did not stop

> your walk in the wood:
> the bluebells
> as you passed
> drew back in comment
> upon an invisible wind
> then nodded forward to stillness.
>
> So brief your old age:
> a project considered
> and quietly rejected.

Someone has died young, that much is clear, and you need no details about the abrupt fatal illness of his wife. In fact there is nothing here, really, to puzzle about, unless you stop to ponder how very refined its simplicity is. In the first three lines it builds its direct, impromptu tone with a list, a swift annotation, as the two-foot lines march off on their walk. The 'prop' is true to its nature, both theatrical and supportive, when it claps together with the only rhyme in the poem. With the bluebells the focus narrows as the lines shorten to a single main stress, gently isolating 'as you passed' for its full weight to register. Then the rhythm modulates into thought, wavering between two main stresses and three but leaning more towards two—'*drew* back in *com*ment'—then more towards three—'u*pon* an in*vi*sible *wind*'—before resolving into trimeter with a clarity that deepens the poise of the image: 'then nodded forward to stillness'. This is a voice that speaks 'quietly' and so much the more tellingly.

To say no more about the poem than that. The chance reader, no longer quite without expectation, might turn a few more pages of *The Entrance to Purgatory*, to see what else this curiosity has to offer—the last part of 'Crusoe's Canoe' perhaps, lifted from its sequence, but then it just happens to be the page you light upon:

> I see something of the art, it has more
> of woman's witchcraft than it has of detail
> a thinking yourself into things. The art
> is to take trees apart in so gentle a way
> that they'll hold themselves together for you
> in a different shape, the living vessel
> that bounces on the waves. It's not about detail—
> it's more like prayer. You have to ask for the shape.
> It's more like love. You have to pity the tree.
> It's more like grief. You have to let things die
> in their own gentle way
>
> to sail off from the island.

And perhaps you are not very disappointed. An *ars poetica*, for a poet working through grief, is a pressing matter: only a sound canoe will carry Crusoe out of his solitude. No critical exposition could capture the essence of Lonie's technique as precisely as the poem itself does: 'to take trees apart in so gentle a way / that they'll hold themselves together for you / in a different shape'. Time and again in his oeuvre he performs this operation with an acute poetic tact, shaping things into metaphorical suggestiveness so delicately that they suffer no violence. 'You have to ask for the shape' he says, even as he shows us why the shape is so significant here: the clipped, direct statements of the last few lines become a series of instructions, a manual of sorts, as if rebuilding one's life after loss requires a return to basics. And then, as the half-lines fall into their balanced, repetitive litany, we realise that they are 'more like prayer' and that the traditional rhythms of supplication and consolation lift the poem into urgency. And we see how these sentences 'hold themselves together'.

These are poems that could have been written yesterday or most of a century ago. Never having been in fashion, they have never gone out of it, and now that the hustling of the seventies and eighties is history, it should be possible to look freshly at Lonie's achievement as the work of one of our enduring contemporaries. The best of his poems have a consummate craft, an intricacy of texture, a sensuous realisation of ideas, all gathered up into an astonishingly direct voice. In singling out a few poems from each collection, I hope to highlight the richness of those textures and also, so far as the scope of a short essay permits, to suggest something of the course of his development and the nature of his engagement with tradition.

Recreations (1967), unsurprisingly for a first collection, lacks the spontaneity of tone that his later poems grow into. It is a young man's book, consciously taut and intellectual, and the poems tend to be grounded conspicuously in a mythical scene or metaphysical apprehension rather than direct experience. Even where myth is absent, the pronominal 'I' and 'he' and 'she' are universalised without, in most cases, any compelling sense of having arrived there through the particular. But if the intellectual impulse is strong, the thinking is also strongly imagistic, with some startlingly vivid lines that rise above mere determination to be poetic and serious.

The first of its three nine-poem sections is preoccupied with the inadequacy of word to world and the poverty of communication in love. No. 2, a sonnet, is typical:

> It may happen at any time, for any cause: your pen
> Falters and stops at the misspelt word; perhaps
> On the table your eye falls on a haphazard stain
> Among the cups, and the talk and the clattering cups
>
> Fade past the thundering curtains of despair;
> And as though behind a wall of glass, lips frame
> Their unechoing words in that remote world where
> You no longer are ...

The sentiment is no novelty, but the articulation is fine enough to convince us at least that he says it because he means it. It is the closing line of the couplet, though, that makes the poem:

> And everything is the same. Such the talk, the table, such.
> Love is the word you hear, the wood you touch.

Love is tongue-tied, the clichéd 'wood you touch', reduced to a superstitious tic, unable to extricate itself from the haphazard stains on the wooden table. And it is also solid, a tangible, homely reality, escaping the echo chamber of words and pervading, in its unspoken way, the domestic scene. It is both 'love' and love. Such casual intensity of meaning is everywhere in his last three collections, and keeps taking us by surprise in his earlier works.

The Recreations of the title suggest, of course, not only play but creating anew. Several of the poems begin from classical mythology, remaking it for contemporaries, and yet they seem at least as drawn to unmaking. Icarus, in No. 12, comes apart, as Icaruses are wont to do:

> The air spread
> Its hands below with love, and bore his light
>
> Limbs upwards beyond cloud and gull
> And the familiar shaped islands, till within
> That ultimate region he found his skill
> And calmly downward, homeward—

But he comes apart with exquisite poise, as if he has discovered the art of dying, an art that in No. 11 belongs to Palinurus, the helmsman of Aeneas, drowned by the gods as sacrifice for the safe passage of his comrades: 'the long green lash / Knotted about my ribs and then unwound / My rolling body to the slow backwash'. The language in these two fatal sonnets verges on erotic, while maintaining a detached, virtually forensic calm, implicit in the balance of the syntax and the deliberative clarity of diction. In No. 19, for instance, the poet tries to reassemble his faculties upon waking: 'legs, unwieldy / As tree trunks must be found and willed through / Sinking distances'. One might even wake without a head,

> beside which elementary panic
> That memories should be settled like distracted birds
> Into an accustomed identity seems mere detail.

His equipoise is deeply aware of fragmentation and failure, seeking to hold it in tension with the possibility of creation, or recreation, and the collection is virtually a manifesto for this aesthetic, an aesthetic he never abandoned but came to inhabit with a more relaxed voice.

Indeed he was already finding his way towards such a voice in the breakthrough poem he chose not to collect. 'Elegy to Maecenas' creates not a symbolic figure but a persona to speak through, and in ventriloquising his poetic concerns he liberates a new dramatic energy:

> In the end, they bring what one wants, the lean obsequious years
> My servants now: it's a young man's way
> To rail at their depredations. I did myself
> Lamenting youth, with not one hair turned grey.

The drama is enriched by the subtle play of identity and irony that the monologue form allows. The speaker's Horatian values—an urbane sensuality, a meditative balance—are certainly living ones for Lonie:

> Yet they read
> My poems still, those civil monuments
> Chiselled from chaos and my catholic lust.
> Therefore, when I am dead
> They will remember the black hair parting above the brow
> Of mad Cinara who once for a whole year

> Burned her hot summer in my aching head
> Till in the end
> I turned her to ash and art.

But they are living only because they are in tension. This is an art built upon ashes, youth consumed along with its exploits, and the youth of others, and the poem is not called an elegy for nothing. Its rhetoric piles up in an attempt at self-persuasion:

> Even that need to boast
> Noted in others sourly, ripened at last
> To an old man's foible, hangs sweet upon the bough.
> All is distinct and calculable gain.

The speaker, of course, protests too much. The occasionally over-ripe tone is quite deliberate, on Lonie's part, and exquisitely controlled. For control is a virtue when it realises what is beyond it. Melancholy is an unspoken presence. 'The shadow of the day / Grows long.'

Letters from Ephesus (1970), aside from its eloquent though abstracted title poem, is less concerned with large ideas than with cultivating a new spontaneity of tone and incisiveness of description. One of its 'Studies', a modest but delightfully celebratory piece, disarms any suspicion of brooding intellectualism:

> In this photograph
>
> I observe two details:
> The collar of your jersey
> From which your neck
> Balancing its sphere of head
> Springs straight as a water jet
> Is so crumpled
> That your smile, aiming at high
> Irony
> Tumbles back into joy.

'I observe': it could preface almost any of his poems from this volume onwards. Always he registers detail with telling precision. Here it is a precision that anatomises and dismembers—reminding us, perhaps, of the danger of waking without a head—even as he pulls the ensemble together again. His habitual aesthetic asserts itself. Only the radiant joy is untypical.

'Street Scene' from the same collection, observing the demolition of a house, is another advance in the art of allowing theme and metaphor to coalesce from the build-up of detail and image:

> Starting
> From inside they gradually
> Hollow it out like an old
> Tooth. There is a skill about it
> Which has to be learned against
> The warped nail and the corroded
> Waste-pipe joint, in all
> Old buildings whose parts conjoin
> To outface destruction.

The skill, whether it be demolition, dentistry or poetry, is forensic:

> There are some things
> Which should never be seen—
> Such as bone. An old couple
> Lived in the flat upstairs
> Rusted together
> Behind the brass pot and the blind.

They should never be seen, but then again they must be, and must be acknowledged. The rusted fusions of suburbia are a recurring element in Lonie's poems, encroaching on his own life as well as others, but when they are pulled apart there may be moments of insight:

> The roof is off, it is luminous within
> And blue sky pours from the windows.
>
> A small crowd gathers
> To see a wall tumble like water.
> Soon a new building
> Will take tenancy of the air.

Poetry's job is to take the roof off, to find the living metaphor in the morbid situation, the sudden synthesis that, coming after patient, meticulous, dissective observation, can flood a poem with light. The light is not always blue and sunny, but it opens up a perspective, a release from the dull pressure of circumstance.

It is notable that Lonie wrote so few dramatic monologues despite the liberation of his talent in 'Elegy to Maecenas'. The poems of *Letters from Ephesus*, as David Howard remarks, offer instead a passive observer, practically a voyeur, a figure who sees and responds but cannot intervene. The dramatic monologue is not a form that readily accommodates this charged marginality, which Lonie clearly sensed was congenial to his voice, even before bereavement made it vital. But a poet of the scope he aspired to must be more than a sensitive presence beyond the picture frame. He was drawn to inhabit the first person more intensely in another of his uncollected watersheds, 'Ugolino and His Sons', a monologue not in a borrowed persona but his own, the Dantean parallel in no way negating the confessional nature of the piece. In fact the tone is bitingly personal: 'My grin a rictus splitting from ear to ear / I drive with half a mind.' Under this pressure the imagery reaches, at its best, a force he had not achieved before:

> We race
> Through the tangle of the streets like wolves:
> Time's tooth is in our flanks, it won't let go,
> Whatever.

Its best is not sustained throughout the poem. The raw emotion behind the verse is patent, perhaps at times too much so:

> Pity stays,
>   Visitant of intolerable, twitching face
>   At the door locked carefully behind your eyes.

Raw emotion is very much the point of course, but for all the deliberate weight of claustrophobia, he had not yet learnt to marry such intensity thoroughly with the incisive meditation that was his poetic second nature. Nevertheless, whether or not it is his most successful early poem, it is certainly the largest, signalling a resolve to face the emotional depths without evasion, while remaining the utterance of a helpless onlooker. In this light it is significant for investing a domestic scene with the full dignity of Dantean reference. Ugolino, imprisoned and starved with his sons and powerless to help them, their compassion turning to reproach, his anguish succumbing to hunger, is an audacious symbol to hang over the poem, but a potent one, all the more effective in being left to resonate without a strained pursuit of the correspondence. The core domestic relations, not in themselves at all grand, are henceforward singled out for high seriousness.

Dante, more importantly than the classical sources of the early verse, was to become a recurring inspiration. *The Divine Comedy* is one of the most pervasive presences in twentieth-century literature, and Eliot's account of his own travails in imitating it may suggest something of its relevance to Lonie:

> It was not simply that I was limited to the Dantesque type of imagery, simile and figure of speech. It was chiefly that in this very bare and austere style, in which every word has to be 'functional', the slightest vagueness or imprecision is immediately noticeable. The language has to be very direct; the line, and the single word, must be completely disciplined to the purpose

of the whole; and, when you are using simple words and simple phrases, any repetition of the most common idiom, or of the most frequently needed word, becomes a glaring blemish.*

Lonie did not seek to imitate, but he found in Dante a permanent validation of his own craft: an austere and pure diction wedded to a strong sensual purchase and a drive for intellectual potency. Like so many other poets, he also found a great overarching structure against which to measure his own integrations and disintegrations, faiths and disbeliefs. And, of course, he found a testament of mourning and the ultimate model of the passionately involved spectator. If we ask ourselves again why the explicit dramatic monologue became a path not taken, the answer may be that he turned instead to a Dantesque first person, in a sense rooted in craft and expanding towards something like a persona, an 'I' with a set of poetic values. That he could never rest quite easy in those values, that he was acutely aware of their limitations, the points at which they break down, rendered many of his poems implicit dramatic monologues of the subtlest kind, with, at times, explicit Dantean reference as an enriching resource. This was to emerge fully in *The Entrance to Purgatory*.

Some poets choose their theme, some find it, others have it thrust upon them. For some it is all three together. Loss and mourning, after the death of Judith Lonie in 1982, became the centre of his poetry and the source of its most powerful statements. The style he had been converging on was well suited to the task that befell it. *Courting Death* (1984) is short, like the two collections preceding it, and its unity of focus renders it more or less a single poetic sequence. As we have seen in the slightly later 'Crusoe's Canoe', the nature of poetry itself is an urgent

---

* T. S. Eliot, 'What Dante means to me', in *To Criticize the Critic* (Faber and Faber, 1965), p. 129.

matter when it is the medium of grief, and the self-reflection of his earlier works deepens in poems like 'Anomalous Behaviour':

> Grief is stronger than fear:
> that much the cock pheasant said
> as we shifted his fluttering mate
> to the roadside and waited for her to die.
>
> His round eye watched us
> as he circled about her, courting death
> we would have said, if that eye
> had not been so opaque
>
> unable to tell us whether grief
> is more than anomalous behaviour, nor
> what changes lay behind the dry-
> stone wall, for mindless birds, for ourselves.

The scene, while quietly arresting, is natural enough, and draws us in with no irritation of contrivance. But the governing image that arises from it is replete with significance: the blind circling distress of the bird is superimposed upon the stately arabesques of a court dance. Grief may be pushed into formality, instinct into form, sight may become the 'round eye' of accomplished poetic vision. And yet the eye remains opaque. Is the poem no more than anomalous behaviour? Does manipulating grief in verse leave us with anything more, in the end, than a stricken monomania? The form itself seems to pose this question in the last stanza with a succession of increasingly sharp enjambments, the lines circling into each other with the restlessness of the anguished bird even as the poem passes into reflection. The mind is a mystery to itself, the 'dry-stone wall' a curtain drawn across it, hinting at grief's aridity and the stony landscape of death's other kingdom, without interrupting the naturalism of the scene. The complexities of the poem come together in 'courting death': to be reckless of death, or to ritualise it, or to make love to it. He has few equals in the art of loading a passing colloquial phrase, or seemingly casual sentence, without breaking the surface clarity and poise.

Among so many fine poems, 'By Foreign Hands' stands out for sheer intensity of feeling:

> You lay in a blue chapel
> under blue sheets drawn to the chin
> your hands not showing.
> Someone else had done your hair
> ignorantly parting
> it on the wrong side.
>
> Someone else had done your hair
> and arranged your hands and tucked you up in bed
>
> and done your hair and done your skin and done your eyes
>
> your long, asymmetrical feet
>
> expertly composing what was to be composed
> expertly parting what was to be parted

The clear blue of heaven collides at the outset with the blue chill of death: the chapel collapses into the clinical expertise of the morgue. Detail does not come more piercing than this: 'ignorantly parting / it on the wrong side'. And then 'tucked you up in bed' is itself tucked in so smoothly that when it explodes we are taken aback by how obscene it is. In the next line, repeating 'done your hair' for the third time, the obsessiveness of grief emerges, and is hammered home: 'and done ... and done ... and done'. She is done for. He cannot have done with her. And the dull repetition lays bare the banality of what can be done: manicuring death. The balance of the last two lines, their deadpan smoothness, is a mockery of the anguish that no poise, no expertise can assuage. Nor are the morticians the only experts in the case: the poet himself is composing and parting, working over asymmetrical feet, and looking back we realise that he too must be 'someone else', one of the morticians. Bereavement is the ultimate exclusion.

If the formal accomplishment of the piece points to its own inadequacy, its inability to transcend emotional disintegration, the expression of that inability is itself a success and a kind of integration. In this paradox, and the tension it generates, the poem is a true descendant of the earlier works. The struggle between form and emotion is more explicitly addressed in 'Cupboard Love':

> Gradually we deplete the larder
> of all the stock you left us.
> Jars are emptied and recycled one by one,
> tawdry packets replace them, sometimes we try
> a new brand, but slowly
> the spaces between them grow. Even the arrangement
> changes: ideas are always the last things to go.
>
> I like the economy of this tidy larder.
> I like things to be used and used up and done with.
>
> What are we to do with your vast untidy love
> that fills every room and corner of this house like the sea
> in a sinking ship and can never be exhausted?

It is not exactly metaphor. It is finely articulated fact saturated with suggestion that coalesces into metaphor. Love gets into things. The bare economy of style enacts the reaching towards a spartan, uncluttered peace. As in earlier poems, though, the constructive impulse is shadowed by a fascination with undoing: dissolution promises renewal, but it is emptiness, not anything positive to replace it, that emerges clearly: 'the spaces between them grow'. The 'you' of the second line frames the poem as a dialogue with the departed, belying the wish for the past 'to be used and used up and done with'. The past inevitably floods back in at the end. This is not, however, a simple negation of the classical 'economy' the preceding lines try to embody. He does indeed 'like' it and it is necessary as well as insufficient. The poem is 'a sinking ship' but not sunk forever: it is forever sinking. He could not have realised this truth to life in poetry if Icarus had not 'found his skill' over a decade earlier. The final *cri de cœur*, even as it seems to overwhelm the formal aspirations of the poem, is cathartic in its formal perfection: the momentum of the single sentence swelling unpunctuated through three lines, the forward surge of the rhythm, tending towards anapaests but never allowed to jog, the drawn out penultimate line that piles noun on noun on noun on noun and flows on into the next, all without straining for effect—insignificant poets cannot do this.

His next collection, *The Entrance to Purgatory* (1986), takes up mourning and remembrance with more meditative distance, although it is a distance repeatedly closed by sharp realisations of the touch of grief. The opening lines of 'Visit' could have served as the volume's epigraph: 'It was too early for such a visit / and it was too late.' It is an extraordinary way to describe a deathbed leavetaking. Now it is too early and too late forever, but between these two relentless verities the poems try, always aware it can only be provisional, to make the right time. I have quoted two of them at the beginning of this essay, and shall dwell here only upon two more.

'The World Outside' takes up the presiding Dantean motif of the volume. Technically virtuosic, this thirty-five-line poem of two sentences, almost every line enjambed, is a *moto perpetuo*, restless and confined:

> This was the last
> vision that you saw, these
> kitchen walls, that familiar

> crack running down, the homely
> cups nodding like madmen
> on their hooks, the blue
> blaze of the gas turned up
> under the kettle, an inward
> fire, a light, a heat
> out of nowhere.

The crack in reality—with its buried suggestion that life is 'running down'—is all the more disturbing for colonising a familiar feature, while the 'homely / cups nodding like madmen', a chorus line of domestic grotesques, lift the ordinary into the extraordinary, even their routine 'hooks' hinting at disturbing Dantesque possibilities. The vision is claustrophobic and something is about to break free. What could have seemed grandiloquent is rendered compelling by the sureness with which metaphysical suggestion arises from concrete scene. Not that there is any heavenly affirmation here:

> You did not see
> that famed mosaic: how it all
> makes sense, fitting
> down to the last
> tessera ...

Instead there is a more elusive promise:

> you did not wonder
> about us, what
> we might think: all that
> arranged beforehand, concealed
> like presents in luggage, or
> just scattered about like clothes
> waiting to be picked
> up in the right order ...

This is the only kind of 'sense' there is to make. The 'arranged beforehand', so horribly untrue with a deeper truth beneath, is a superb touch: mundane love is all there is and it must discover its own providence retrospectively and yet in a sense, unlike the other kind, it may be a true providence. But not an easy one. The concluding lines pursue the 'vision' to the point of dissolution:

> the blue-edged hole opening
> the outside world at last
> and a night that had swallowed
> its own stars.

And here the Dantean subtext surfaces clearly in its negation. It is he, after all, who imagines her vision, and at the point of loss there is no *primum mobile* left, no love that moves the sun and other stars, and the vision folds in upon itself.

'The Entrance to Purgatory' is the volume's conclusion and summation. It is built upon Dante more intrinsically than any of his other poems, with the antipodean Mount Purgatory as sustained analogy for the poet's decision to leave Europe—the 'dead vista / of northern cities which have lost their hearts for ever'—and return to New Zealand, specifically to Dunedin, etymologically 'city on a hill' and in its origins a Free Church settlement. To die in grace is to choose grace, and to live in any sort of grace before death, religion aside, is no less so:

> You are glad to be here, when it would have been so easy
> at the last moment simply to permit
> the past its habitual choice: blind, heavy-handed
> and hopeless in its passion.

But to wrest choice away from the dead hand of habit requires moral clarity, and that in turn draws upon a more basic purity of perception and speech:

> What you will notice first is the air's
> greater clarity: you had not remembered
> how it gave to trees the instructive simplicity
> of a botanist's drawing.

This is an acute response not only to the quality of southern light, but to the supremely lucid articulation of Dante's verse, the exaltation it achieves not through vagueness but through precision, and the poem locates this as a fundamental of grace. Not, of course, literally religious grace—Lonie distances himself from both Catholic and Calvinist:

> Those whiskered bigots who planned
> this city in holy ignorance of its terrain
> meant it a cradle of virtue, but perhaps you must
> return here more than once, your suitcase crammed
> with disappointments and leading loss by the hand
> to learn how insistently its ways will bring
>
> you always to one point, until their choice becomes
> your second nature.

The choice to return was, among other things, a choice to devote himself to poetry, including the progressive purgatory of grief that art became for him, and this is a large part of what the city represents. It is place as well as symbol, though, and landscape realised in poetry will, the final lines promise, help return poetry to the 'instructive simplicity' of the opening:

> Here too the city will help, hill tree and tower
> by sunlight or by starlight assembled into a setting
> for something to take place in, a place to go on from.

Built upon that simplicity, and sustained throughout the poem, is an extraordinary achievement in meditative verse: the balance and clarity of articulation are faultless, yet never precious or over-refined, for the poem continuously thinks, at a creative stretch of which the poise is a symptom, and thinks urgently enough to take up in its draught a considerable weight of meaning, in which the intensely personal merges, with full conviction, into some of the central tropes of Western culture. These spacious verse paragraphs, fluid but measured, mark Lonie's arrival at the height of his maturity and anticipate the most remarkable poems of his final collection.

Winter Walk at Morning (1991), his last and posthumously published collection, takes up a broader range of themes and a more explicit engagement with New Zealand. There is nothing in it that is not subtle and finely wrought, but two poems in particular stand out as major orchestrations. 'Ancestral Ground' unfolds in four long meditative stanzas, describing what appears to be a crematorium, although a vague indefiniteness on that point reflects the sterility of our treatment of death, our failure to look at it squarely:

> These places that seem half factory, half—what?
> —spacious like power houses, glassed clear
> leaving no corner for misery to breed ...

Without speaking its name, without naming its function, he anatomises the face it presents with his customary precision:

> one curtain wall, clad in cheerful brick
> suspends a slim and lightly varnished cross
> dividing us from the room next door—that window too high
> to see through ever—gravel swept bare
> to its concrete base: stations tended with municipal care.

Never mind what happens in the room next door. That 'ever' lifts the telling detail into something like indictment, with the utmost economy. And the parenthesis nudges us towards the suggestion that the cross itself, a meagre municipal Christianity, is a window one is not really meant to look through. The setting is no help:

> This one's different only by being perched
> on the land's edge. You could look miles away
> from the blonded oak, out where the sea
> slides smoothly in, its silken rollers
> a faint blue-grey; or, if it's spring
> to the gorse that blossoms gold along the cliffs;
> and think if you like of hats and dresses
> or the colour of eyes or of anything
> but these decent faces turned lumpy with tears
> and hands knotting on the backs of chairs.

It is not in the landscape but on the edge of it, 'perched' awkwardly, and to look at the view is to 'look miles away'. The building does not humanise the landscape. The landscape does not touch the experience of those in the building. The view is not even a distraction in its own right but a vacant space for the projection of other distractions. This is where the dead bury their dead:

> Outside in the carpark the assembled rows
> of cars are waiting, each different and all the same,
> to drive away soon; and beyond the cars, the same
> grey slabs repeated in orderly rows.
> There's a quiet rumbling somewhere, as though
> a river fell through turbines far below.

Rhyme collapses into repetition. The 'quiet rumbling somewhere' is entirely verisimilar, yet suggestively vague, even as it eases into metaphor: we try to contain and sterilise, but there are depths, and things will go on in them, however debased and interrupted. The final shift into direct statement has been patiently earned:

> I think most of our poverty that contrives
> such poor space to unvest ourselves of lives:
> heads bent in shame, hands that unknot and unbutton
> and knot up again to go out and on:
> all caught in the homely legend that turns around
> this abstract space, our one ancestral ground.

The hands, detached more or less from any persons seen whole, take us back to the unravelling bodies of *Recreations*, unknotting and unbuttoning with an air of moral collapse, but the knotting up again offers no countervailing recreation, merely a grim buttoned-up inarticulacy. The 'homely legend' of Christianity is indeed a mere homely legend, displaced from home. It leaves us with death as a naked abstract space.

In acknowledging such deracination, Lonie was far from implying that it is universal or insurmountable. Poems such as 'Proposal at Allans Beach' make this clear enough:

> But up there above the ridges
> it's always going on: the air
> dividing, and pouring mist
> down ngaio gullies, making sheep
> get up and move, unveiling contours
> taking them away again.

To realise place so vividly is 'to see how we match up / to its absolute background' and thus to reveal, and perhaps assimilate, the past and the dead: 'the place is full of ghosts'. But the frequent poverty of the spaces we have contrived is not the less a fact to be faced, at least as much because of when we live as where, and the title poem of the collection confronts this challenge head on.

'The Winter Walk at Morning' invokes William Cowper's long poem *The Task*, conflating the titles of Book V (The Winter Morning Walk) and Book VI (The Winter Walk at Noon). He places himself in the tradition of Cowper's meditative melancholy, but the Nature that consoled his eighteenth-century predecessor has become an anti-pastoral travesty. The walker stumbles in the idiomatically awkward title. The 'at Morning' may also be a glance at the allegorical proclivities of the moralising Cowper, but if the title is playful, the scene itself appears in devastating earnest:

> Out there where the spilled city began
> to crumble at its edges into a spatter of
> one-time village names (though any quaint
> feature of architecture or sweet natural
> touch was now half crusted over or floating in
> development, a sort of adaptable
> homogeneous flow, vivid like bile) ...

Is this Morning in New Zealand or a post-industrial British twilight? That we cannot be sure is in itself a rather dismal circumstance. Standing upright? 'Walk, why walk? Nobody goes for walks here.' As always with Lonie the level-headed clarity contains a build-up of pressure:

> why
> should one start to think of raped corpses here, why
> should the fluttering loops of surveyor's tape remind
> of bloodstained bandages, looped along battlefields?

The more closely one looks at this landscape, the less it belongs to 'the calm-browed / reasonableness of things'. The penultimate stanza hints at a Dantesque landscape of lost souls but seems finally more like a sort of debased *Kubla Khan*:

> I hesitated, then crossed the field. To souls
> no definite place is granted. I was not told
> I should find the river, but there it was

> flowing, apparently, between low floodbanks
> from a bend up there, where were some low trees
> to disappear again under the motorway
> that came into sight now, barring other progress.

'Barring other progress': the suppressed, sometimes thwarted emotion is not just a personal matter but increasingly a reflection on the poet's environment and nation. The final stanza brings this home definitively:

> Undeniably a river, with a river's purpose
> and the purposes we find for rivers, as: to be the end
> of a winter morning's walk, or to sit down
> and weep by, or just chuck rubbish into:
> about midstream were two cars
> like dead crabs upside down exposing shafts
> and exhausts. Their celebrated river was nothing, then:
>
> not deep enough even to bury a wrecked car.

The 'celebrated' landscape, on which we are apt to congratulate ourselves, is often what we have contrived to make it, and often it reflects our poverty. So restrained, so unforced is the tone of the verse that it is easy not quite to notice its audacity: 'to sit down and weep by, or just chuck rubbish into'. Or as Psalm 137 has it, 'By the rivers of Babylon, there we sat down, yea, we wept, when we remembered Zion.' It is obvious how very private the melancholy of this winter walker is—he has his own wreck to bury—and we may be startled to find it co-opting the communal voice of the Bible, a contrast that perhaps even deepens our sense of its privacy, until we begin to reflect on the communal loss, and loss of community, implied in the landscape. To 'just chuck rubbish into': to grasp how finely calculated this is, consider how much weaker the line would be without the 'just'. It is the most exquisitely casual of outrages.

In the late uncollected 'Not a Poem' Lonie complains he is unable to write 'straightforward' poetry, 'simple / as folksong'. The big themes tease him into contemplation:

> and I find I need a string quartet
> and centuries of civil culture
> not to speak of philosophy and foreign languages.

An intellectual's nostalgia for the irreducibly simple is likely enough to be sincere. But he could be, and often was, penetratingly direct, and none of his poems are burdened with a modernist clutter of more or less obscure reference. They do not strive to get culture in. Instead they speak out of it, as well as out of immediate experience, and fuse those two elements. Indeed very few New Zealanders, perhaps none besides Baxter, have written so many good poems possessed of an urgent inner necessity. His ironies are neither coy nor solipsistic. At the heart of this urgency is an unflinching treatment of domestic life that began to emerge even before the bereavement that became central to it. In this Lonie was well ahead of his compatriots. As the private and domestic move closer to the centre of New Zealand poetry, he could well be taken as exemplary, and all the more so for the 'centuries of civil culture' that no other New Zealand poet, not even Curnow and certainly not Baxter, has so vitally assimilated. These are the peers with whom he belongs, and there are not so many such achievements in our literature that we can afford to neglect one of them. When he becomes, as he surely will, a place to go on from, he will cease to read like a forgotten conscience.

Wellington, January 2015

I ∾ Digging to the Antipodes

And as a child I thought
Of digging to the Antipodes
To enlarge my back-yard world.

—'Remarks on a Landscape Painting'

'RUBBING MY HAND ALONG THE ROUGH-CAST WALL'

Rubbing my hand along the rough-cast wall
   Of some suburban home
I think of palaces that have been built.
The flaking paint catches, clogging in my finger nails
   Or flutters downwards in a yellow fall.

Spread out against the wall, waiting for the whip
My hand is gravel scored and grooved.
With stone as silken as the marble lip
   Of Cleopatra's sphinx
They built a palace by the Nile.
Foam-white stone, and like a goddess' foot
Laced beneath with delicate blue veins.
   But spit, and smile
And build your palace from the stones along the beach.

[MS-3619/027]

'NOW SPRING DAWNS IN OUR MONTHS OF PASSION'

Where drowsy limbs a treasure keep
    —Auden

Now spring dawns in our months of passion
Hand and upturned face
Seek for the sun, and warm
Your limbs a treasure yield

Wandering on the mountain's side
Pluck the green leaf, hear the bird
While this slim blade nods

Love, remember still
Serene the peaks, unchanging

Now spring dawns in our months of passion.

[MS-3619/034]

'THE FISHERMAN'S LINE STARTLED'

The fisherman's line startled
The dull air, easily falling into
A white look and the still river

And it was in his hand a daring
Conjecture at an alien world
Down there where light failed

[MS-3619/027]

SOLSTICE

Sunday afternoon. The week hung wavering
And fickle, we forgot each others' smell.
Down at Girvan the boss was savouring
Salt and seaweed, perhaps in an open necked shirt—
We wished him joy of it: this was our holiday.
From the hills, Glasgow's dirt
Pleasantly hazed her haphazard jumble:
Shut self to all but the sunful mumble.

Sleep the typewriters beneath black covers
Children sail yachts and feed the swans.
That day we could even forgive the lovers
Though they hope to get married on four-ten a week
Though their home be a hovel, their one child a freak.

[September 1948, MS-2674/105, variant MS-3619/027]

ALLARDYCE

> ... *the body pointed straight in the direction of the island, and the compass read duly E.S.E. and by E.*
> *'I thought so,' cried the cook; 'this here is a p'inter.'*
> —*Treasure Island*

By rust of weapon
And rotten cloth surrounded
His bones lay vainly arched.
Coarse blade and stalk, root swollen
Strove into the crowded song
Of brittle and black-veined wing.
Above that island, leaves moved in sun:
Their pattern slid smoothly away.
As silently back, down the long bone.
Allardyce, undoubtedly pointing some way.

[MS-2674/105, variant MS-3619/027]

FRAGMENT

O where are you now, my Hebrides
In a crowded noon of summer?
We wished winter away, forgetting
How the trees stood bare
How the seas grew wild, casting
About under a ragged sky;
How the rock spoke danger.

[MS-2674/105, MS-3619/027]

HOLIDAY NOTES

1 *Evening*

Laughing, we landed and lugged the boat
Slow up the shingle, dug in the anchor
Mindful of sudden storm and shifting wind;
Stacked our gear, and walked home, hands
Blistered and legs tired.
Now we sit, Don writing a letter, his nib
The only sound; my head too tired
To remember adolescent anxieties.

2 *Morning*

I smoke, drink, read, watch the sky
And glumly, the hours pile up
—Crumbs, cups, stubs, books,—by the bed
Unattractive, untidy their death.

While mist on the hills, warm as settler's breath
Hangs now among wet bracken
And the softness of grey water to the rain
Promotes a Hebridean outlook.

Which I am thankful for, But oh
Sodden skies, when shall I break a
Bright day, like water on the clear lake,
Dive down, and touch the stones?

3 *Night Passage*

Since we two happened together
At this time and at this place
You turned, carrying your careless
Desire to me, your willing neighbour.

—Leaving the launch, to leeward
Seas rolled into the night;
Someone touched a guitar, light-
ly the lonely sang.

For hours you lay in my shoulder;
My smile found that it searched
In your face, and there rested
As our hands in each other:

Since at this time and at this place
We two happened together.

[January 1949, MS-2674/105, variant MS-3619/027]

TARAWERA

Pines glide their green glacier down
To the lake, cupped, and cold
To the blood of animals; who fear,
Shyly part fringing reeds,
Delicately drink. Summer, winter

No men come, carrying gear
Or in empty-handed worship
Where this mountain, rising by spur
Saddle and scored flank, lifts up
Its silent head, and competes with stars.

[MS-3619/027]

'WHY WILL YOU STAND SO, AGAINST THE
   WINTER SKY'

Why will you stand so, against the winter sky
Where all the winds adore you on this hill
So careless in perfection?—ah, beauty
Is merely simple to the beautiful.

Yet can you, when you turn to kiss me there
Forgive the sudden agony in my eyes
Who cannot love you as the winds love, dear—
Hurt with desire I shall not realise.

[MS-2674/105]

SONG

Ah, little use, now that I'm bleeding
To fly your sight, your body's touch;
For love's gaunt gunmen, never ceasing
Track down the one who knows too much.

Casual did the flesh surrender:
What secrets were, to love confessed?
And if I will, farewell for ever
The beauty by my arms possessed.

But treacherous under nights of beauty
Had love unlocked a novel tongue:
Oh, must I ever miss my own heart,
Bearing thine till love be done?

[May 1950, MS-2674/105]

BY A RIVER

And was it here, six months ago
Our hearts were with such summer crossed?
Now darker does the river flow
And I return alone, and lost.

But waiting still, I listen, peer,
As if time could his steps retrace
Until your kisses found my mouth
Your hair flowed all about my face.

Yet I'm a dreaming fool, I swear
To hope such miracle could be:
That time, whose motley lovers wear
Reverse his mockery for me.

[MS-2674/105]

SONNET

Now one has gone from me, and coming night
Joins with my grief to rain in hopelessness
Strip naked my warm heart and force it out
To shudder in its native wilderness—
Though each must brave the ordinary trial
For permanence from day to day must grope
Though heaven itself, that makes love possible
Conspire to take again its granted hope
—Let our minds change not with our bodies' place
Nor time work in our hearts his treachery;
Find still engendered, in each stranger face
Our love, that grows from all humanity;

The nightly prayer be speech, and understood;
And all our memory, of another's good.

[August 1950, MS-2674/105]

SCOTTISH MILL TOWNS

Their names uncouth on the tongue as flint
These lie at the valley's broadening
Couched in mild hills. The striding
Shepherd sees from above, unexpectedly,
A dark tide of women, shawled,
Disturb the sharp air with chatter
As clogs farewell morning down frosted streets
To where the mill, a giant Minotaur
Already pants and rumbles from a Grecian yield.
Higher in the valley, sheep
Flanks still dew heavy, by the same stream crop,
Where with joy the morning cascades down from the shining
    fields.

[1951, *Otago University Review 1888–1971*, variant MS-3619/027]

'GIVE TO ALL YOUTH THIS I HAVE KNOWN'

Give to all youth this I have known:
    Attaining the ridge,
    Met with the upswept wind
Panting a little, with his own
Exertion and the praising mind.
Was surely blindness, seeing only the next stone?

Only the scratched hand peeling
Only his eyes to the ground?
But balanced on scarp, his eyes would widen,
Turn face to wind, hair backwards blowing
Now by his laughing power hidden
To conquer the long plain, forward thrown.

Finally sure, being young he shall conquer.
Let him: his doom rides in triumphal cars
   For though at the end, the populace cheering
Defeated is conqueror, and wise to the cheers.
So let him climb, his hands scarring
And pause at the ridge, untouched in power

Hold him a moment, then let him go leaping.

[MS-3619/027]

'AT WHORING I WAS INEFFECTUAL'

At whoring I was ineffectual
And so became an intellectual.

[MS-3619/027]

LETTER FROM A DISTANCE

To you, my dear, my thoughts go from this bed
As I imagine how you'll set a light
To greet me home, across wind-darkened waters

While I, by chance, lie in a distant bed
Though unextinguished that lamp lay its light
Till dawn shall dowse it, over unseen waters.

Crude were the joys that made our nuptial bed,
Ignored the appeal of your most intimate light
For understanding: wilder grew the waters

Whipped by the wind from our disordered bed.
Till we might wake to day's deceiving light
Our private tears we drowned in sleep's own waters.

So, now, it seems we knew no common bed
But strove in dreams, each to a separate light,
While gross limbs ever sank through nightmare's waters.

Though our desire should never know that bed
Where limbs' brief touch flares forth a world of light
Whose substance swings beyond the envious waters,

Still must I search, till in a narrower bed,
Unfound my fancied world, your proper light,
I lose both in death's separating waters.

[*Landfall* Volume 6 Number 3 September 1952]

WICKLIFFE BAY

The Sea Fog

After the dark had come, the wind dropped suddenly,
Strangely. Outside my probing light
Met only fog, dank as a dungeon wall.
And showed where macrocarpas, more dark than night

Hunched like the seven sins about my house.
Lying in bed that night, I heard the sea
Swathed by the fog, roll like a mourning drum,
And the foghorn warning, that seemed to me

To beat time to the funeral march of doom.
Then as the small mouse turned in the wainscoting
Fear turned within me, and gnawed
At my heart as I lay there, listening

All night to the ancestral voice that speaks
Through lips curved in the baboon's grin
Till I knew well those dim lineaments
And my soul's antiquity of sin.

Yet, walking this morning, I met a world
More white than winter's; and at peace
I stood there, seeing the fog that lay
Like a benediction upon the trees.

The Hay Field

It is the first day of winter now,
    And the first for me:
I stand here, watching the evening rush
Like some hunted beast from the sea
    And its cold shadow fall
    On this hayfield like a pall.

And I muse that it is not long
    Since the hare
Ran with his mate through the friendly grass
Of this paddock, now lying bare
    While the grey rain weeps
    And down the stack-side seeps.

Remembering the brown-lipped reapers
    And the look of ale
Poured amber in the fecund sun

I shiver at touch of the rising gale
    From the south stinging bleak
    Like a whip on my cheek.

And as I look at the hollow
    Stubble about my feet
Now cloud after cloud sweeps over the hill
I cry aloud for pain of the sweet
    Spring blades that must
    Through the stubble thrust.

Till, turning at last from the fury
    That drums on my back
I go to my house that crouches
Low under the low cloud-wrack
    Knowing too well the pain
    Of death, and beginning again.

Morning Calm

After the storm is past, I hear the sea:
The wind's dropped in my trees, and in this cove
A gull sleeps on smooth water. Still the wave
Goes ramping on the outer shore, will not let be
The vagrant drift. Last night, my Lord, in me
Your storm shook, and the spring-tide of your love
Drew all my heart's parched bones into that grave
To find their quietness under that sea.

And yet this morning, all's too calm. Again
I wander aimless, drifted from your ways,
And wander may, till time upon me preys.

Landlocked I lie, and find no seaward lane,
Compelling current. Thy storm beats in vain
Until its restless power surge through my days.

[1952, *Otago University Review*, variant MS-2674/105]

LETTER FROM A FERRY

   to D.F.M.

In the old days there would have been banquets to propitiate
The sea-gods, there would have been keening of women
   And the presentation of lucky charms
   Against drowning and fever:

Now with nonchalance we enter the gaping vessel
As though for each it were really a fragment of time, not
   A leap into darkness, a severing of all
   We have unredeemably been.

Yet as I wander lost through the inhuman corridors
Encountering those who are united only by chance and a common
   Bewilderment, death, I imagine,
   Would be something like this.

Meanwhile, quietly as from a belief the steamer has slipped
From the wharf, and outstripping the dark hills, sways
   Already to the oceanic rhythm.
   The southerly, harping

Its archaic mode in steel rigging to some is reminiscent
Of a long-foundered people who sailed with grace and daring
   The Aegean, but prized chiefly
   The plainlands with their horses,

Hating the black ocean which unamenable to our nostalgia
Is neither beautiful nor romantic, but an enigma
    Only the unhealthy desire to contemplate,
    The hubristic to answer.

Most of us, however, lonely and a little anxious, wait
As long as we can in the bar's superficial warmth
    With drinks to mirror the extravagant desires
    We do not communicate.

So one who lost his nerve in the confounding cities
Sits before me with nervous eyes and fidgeting hands:
    For him the homestead on the plains,
    The poplars and the gentle

River that taught his limbs their boyhood courage.
A salesman, brimful of whisky and good resolutions
    Returning once more to a blasé wife
    Vows he will open up

New areas of sympathy and sensation. The sanguine envisage
Fresh jobs with richer prospects; youth a wild fortnight
    Of expensive thrills and cheap affection
    In the Delightful City.

Some, it is true, have nothing to anticipate,
But sadly recalling a face and a gesture, brood
    On time's brutality and the facile
    Promises of lovers,

But not here at the point of departure does sorrow stalk
Like a bully among the constructive children, but in the drab
    Morning crowds he welcomes us
    With a deceitful kiss.

Meanwhile the lights go out and sleepers around me
Are perhaps for a time made happy. Lying here
   No more than an arm's-length from the ocean
   I hear its wisdom mutter:

'False your vision, who with the panic of birds
Skimming nightly over my depths, see only a barrier
   To the Edens you would re-inhabit:
   Yet in your dreams I enter,

Or when the elaborate fugue has faded, and in the silence
You are aware of the disorder that nurtures all harmony:
   You have only to ask: O will you not dare
   The years of wrath and thunder.'

[MS-2674/105]

IDIOT'S SONG

God alone knows all my mind
   But God won't tell:
The world's yellow oyster oozes with sunlight.
   God's the empty shell.

(Have a beer, have a beer, Charlie)

More years ago than my grandfather remembers
   The world began to breed:
The white maid lay with a handsome snake
   And a clock stopped at the deed.

(Morning and evening come
   the schoolgirls gay as blackbirds)

So now I must sing a shapeless song
    And offer all who pass
Through thirsty creation an invisible drink
    From a non-existent glass.

(Have a beer, have a beer, Charlie)

All day I watch the sunlit street
    From whence shall come my aid:
Around two corners the angels sing—
    My song ends with a spade

(Morning and evening come
    the schoolgirls gay as blackbirds)

The schoolgirls shall all sing naked there
    Stripped of their black disguise
While sun and moon in fear drop down
    And the stars put out their eyes.

(Have a beer, have a beer, Charlie)

But serpent and maid must mate again
    Ere I lie where I belong.
God is the drink, the empty belly,
    The form of my shapeless song

(Have a beer, have a beer, Charlie:
    Have a beer).

[MS-2674/105]

from REMARKS ON A LANDSCAPE PAINTING

Peace and quiet may be sought
'At the still point of the turning world'
And as a child I thought
Of digging to the Antipodes
To enlarge my back-yard world.

Then gave it up, merely because
Not seeing that one might turn
I had no skill to walk on my hands.
Through the world's hollowed axle now I gaze
But cannot make that turn.

[MS-2674/105]

THE REAL McCOY

Some men have never had the fire
But had all else which men desire
And went so far, but reached no higher.

From all that has been made and sung
Not one drop of blood is wrung
To suffuse with fire a pedant lung.

One among thieves and robbers fell
Starved and beaten, lay in hell,
Writing profusely but not well.

No patent regimen, no diet
Nor learning, meditative quiet
Nor drink nor lechery can buy it.

Lantier the authentic vision had
But all he painted turned to bad
—Daubing and daubing till he was mad;

And Arnold had a love affair
In Switzerland—the guts weren't there;
Coleridge scribbled on in despair.

And I would add McGonagall
But that he had no vision at all
—To fail completely is not to fall.

Though we would let our hero be still
Lacking the vision or the skill
—The muse is a wayward goddess still.

[MS-2674/105]

LIFER

The tree of life may grow outside your cell
And you never can come nearer than the wall;
Its presence gives you some idea of hell,
But thank your stars you have a tree at all.

It's not a file that slips between those bars
No chisel that can work that granite loose,
Though something passes from its world to yours.
You've time to meditate upon its use.

Your meals as regular as clockwork come
To measure out your day; the leaves renew.
His diet and his knowledge of the times
That make man what he is, may keep you, you.

Keep your cell tidy and observe the rules
Until your minor sentence is completed.
If that's your object, only time can school
You in those means whereby time is defeated.

[MS-2674/143]

WITCH

Look, said she, who can remember all things
(When she has a mind to it) a witch must learn
Taking my hand in hers, she said Look
When I command it, fire will not burn.

And laid it trembling upon the bright embers
—She watching the fire, I her firelit face
(Who can perform all things when she remembers)—
Till I heard it crackle in a sudden blaze.

I looked to see something like blackened wood—
It was this old hand alright, and not the same:
But flexing my fingers in that confirmation
Felt in their knotted joints the green sap flame.

[MS-2674/143]

from 'THE ROSE-TREE IN MY GARDEN GREW
    SUDDENLY STILL'

1

The rose-tree in my garden grew suddenly still
As if it had learned to support the weight of its blossom
Only by standing perfectly still in the soft earth.

The hedgehog heard my step and remained perfectly quiet
His button eye uncommunicative as the moon.
Time brimmed around us in the clear well of my garden.

   2

To become acquainted, to know—how is that possible?
It happens every minute. To turn away, to forget,
In sleep or death to watch knowledge plummeting
Forever away from us to unknown depths—that too.

   3

Between tree and hedgehog there's a kind of understanding,
Being half plant himself, with his woody mouth
And untidy spine. How heavy he sits on the earth
Like a small cannon ball someone had dropped there
And proved thereby a natural affinity.

[MS-2674/143]

THE ACHAEANS

Two sonnets from a sequence

   1

Their forefathers, moving through a fluent
World of winds and rivers, forests and storms
Saw life as movement, death as other movement,
Lived undisturbed, till they observed what forms

The wind made as it brushed the mountain side
And the river made as it swirled under the rock
—Dim permanences under the Protean tide—
And gave them names, and understood their talk

And mated with them. One was born of the sea,
Tall demigod, fated to die too soon
Wore something of its salt austerity

Stiff on his brow and lips, and sailed alone
The grey wastes of his mind and understood
Death as no human, no immortal could.

2

Towards the dawn, slow Orion turned
Down to the sea and Greece, and sentries slept.
Between the dull fires and the wall a wind
Sprang up and smoothed the clotted sands and swept

Round the long burial mounds. The slack
Hellespont turned and filled and without noise
Sent its dark waters up the beach to lick
The prows of vessels painted red like toys.

Lying on straw, their women would retrace
Sleeplessly the shape of tent and hut
Unfamiliar rough thigh, bearded face,

And wonder how those knotted hands could fit
With delicacy the lyre's thin cord and sing
Of death with such evident understanding.

[early 1958, 63691 MS-0996-002/221]

ELEGY, ARMIDALE CEMETERY

1

They lie so quiet.
                      The mouth is stopped at last
With the dust of its own eloquence and through their eyes
Earth within stares into earth beyond.
There is no sound here, that is not the sound
Made by the living, who from stones spell out
The names of what is nameless, or the dates
Of those whose time is now and never, the prayers
Of those who have no wish for prayer, they lie
So quiet.
           And yet we name them, yet we pray.

2

I give them back their names, remark their prayers
Am made uneasy by the smaller graves, by those
Who carried with them such small store of words
Their death was not included. And by
The fenced grave with the rusted bolt, whose same
Self-fructifying weed has sourly grown
Withered and grown and withered more summers now
Than any care to recall.
                       By this, by these
And on another grave some crumbling shells
Are drawn into a cross that oddly straggles
As though the hand that patiently set them there
Had to atone for what it still betrayed,
Some habitual awkwardness.

                    By these, by any signs
That death may come too early or too late
May leave much space between the dead and the living
That all our birds die in that birdless air.

3

It is spring now, the season for sap to press
With urgency along these twisted boughs
Up, down, then up again—the blossoming season
When time breaks through time's cortex, ringing it round
In a deliberate slumber ossified.
O season of the hard and soft, your colours burn
With the clarity of loss.
                              Below me on the highway, a truck whines
Southward, then fades, is gone. A lizard shams
Its leather death. The warm wind stirs
And the heart rejects its sorrow. The wind stirs
And touches my temples softly with time's completion.

4

Do the dead stay untouched by season—whether
These bones that lie side by side, but may not
Turn to each other as in sleep or the act
We call by love, and can mean sharing (if
They see at all, it is only upwards and outwards
Though further between the stars than we can see)
—Whether these bones are the artefact that life
Wove on its loom of flesh, contemplation wore
Understanding wore, love wore, and then discarded,
Or whether they are the loom itself, does spring

Touch them no longer there, and do they feel
My footsteps fall now less than the encircling bark
Feels the run of the sap it guards and guides
Or feels the bud that ruptures it at last?

   5

Man, woman, buried child meet in me here
Standing where two gravelled paths intersect
Under the cypress, by the forgotten grave
And their wish that endures on stone finds repetition
Upon my tongue, finds its requital there
Upon my soft and mortal tongue—
                              the dead
And the living are one, as a tree is one
In which the sleeved sap stirs,
                          the ocean
Recalls a voice among its leaves, and sings
Between its branches
Night hangs its eternal constellations.

[September 1958, MS-2674/143]

'PERHAPS IT IS ITS DEATH'

Perhaps it is its death that fascinates,
Or simulation of life, its vivid hair
Streamed backward from your bird-like skull: desire
From tip to root no cell communicates.

Flesh will answer flesh: the hand entreats
The thigh assents, despite us. I despair
Who lie and fumble for your will, and fear
Your body's answer, which the will negates.

Safer to read the moral from your eyes
Which tell how worthless giving and receiving
And gaze elsewhere. So, lest your body feign

And I believe, I stroke your hair that lies
Across my hand, insensate, undeceiving

And the aimless wind fumbles upon the pane.

[*Landfall* Volume 13 Number 1 March 1959]

DIALOGUE

St Peter: Have you ever done anyone any good in the course of your life?

I: No.

St Peter: Can you advance any reason to show that it was better for you to be born than not to be?

I: No.

St Peter: Have you succeeded in what you tried to do?

I: No.

St Peter: In that other, quite different, limited sphere where you might have done some good—have you succeeded there?

I: I failed to admit its existence until too late.

St Peter: Can you advance any reason whatsoever why you should be admitted?

I: I have constructed a card index.

St Peter: Enter.

[12 August 1960, MS-3619/035]

'ONCE AGAIN I RECOGNISE THAT COAST BLACK AS IRON'

Once again I recognise that coast black as iron
Notable stepmother to ships, its peaks clouded with rain;
But once inside her harbours, famous for spring mildness,
For softness of arms on shoulders scabbed and welted
By salt and scurvy, for the depth and dark of her fountain of life

Mother and wife, she makes men voyagers still
That love may draw them more deeply into her earth
Under the roots of her trees, adding their lymph to her streams,
Releasing their voices, each indistinguishable
In the music heard at night among her mountains.

For her love thrives on love, on those she embraced and buried;
Their hearts too simple, their need too urgent for jealousy.
So I too hope, at the lightest touch of her streams
At the slow caress from head to foot of her airs
To recover innocence blank as the unbroken shell.

As if a kiss or whisper could unmake ten years—
The whistle and smack of sudden outrage, the slow
Discoloration of time, as if these things could be forgotten:
Not even in her fires can the old grow young again
The experienced put off knowledge bought with their ruined skins.

One should ask something else of her perhaps: not love,
The ring made perfect again in the swift illusory furnace.
Tired of generous giving, she at last demands her price:
That her sons and lovers bear their scars proudly
Back to her earth, salting with wisdom its large innocence.

For her coast that heaves there now does not belie her nature.
We were deceived: the white surface of innocence
Was formed of her air and water, if for anything
That time might write more legibly such thoughts
As sound at night from peak to peak, in her fires, in her ice.

This is her austerity; that her waters refuse to give now
What they gave: her depths dry and forever sealed,
Her iron shoulders humped away from the wayfarer.
Her generosity, to the one knowledge we did not seek:
No voyage may end, no real possession be discarded.

So I salute her, who sent us forth with empty hands
And receives us with no comfort but appraisal;
Her grey stare kinder than any smile, as the wind yells from
    her peaks
A bleak intelligence, that our only answer
Is our question itself, made simple by loss, made exact by pain.

[MS-2674/143]

'HAVING TAKEN THAT DECISION, YOU COULD NOT SEE'

Having taken that decision, you could not see
Any change in his habits, or speech.
His friends reported
No public acts of worship, no eccentricities

Of the inopportune: there was nothing to praise
And time did not alter its character.
The miracle was, he was largely unaware.

He continued as before: if it had cost
Any sacrifice, to the fires of love and rage,
Of the loved and hated, the loveless now, it would have shown
In the lines of his face, those normal to his age.

It meant nothing. Had you asked, he could not have said
How it was that the furious landlocked waters had broken
To run thereafter in the care-deepening bed.

[MS-2674/143]

from 'AS THE GREY RIVER BROUGHT ME
   ROUND AGAIN'

As the grey river brought me round again
I thought I saw you on the bank.
                              You held
Your own shape among the others there, distinct
As I had seen you once, and see you now.
It was strange. You did not recognise me there.
I saw my shredded, sodden body in your stare.

[MS-2674/143]

THE FORCED LISTENER

  for C.B.

Thinking of you—but have you not said enough
Yourself, of the scope of such thinking? Its casual
Vain impertinence, yes, and as well
Its crying need—for what else have you, have we
To write about? Only by person, place or thing
The devious routes of the other

Do we come to ourselves, that were lost.
                              This is the conundrum
The puzzling artefact, undated, unrelated
Or natural stone of strange, symbolic meaning
Held in your hand, turned over and over for years
Until, last night
Suddenly lightened, you seemed to toss it among us
And watched with irony and affection to see
What we would make of it.

Let me say it, then: surrounded
By friends you seemed one much alone
Chosen by fate or fortune to attend
To that unnerving silence, its haunting absence
Of person and thing, all loneliness of mirrors
And ticking clocks, blank stare of paper
Absence (finally) of ourselves, and of that land
In which our selves find meaning—
                              Encountered
Whether in city garden or forest of mountain beech
The first matter of all our eloquence
Which our eloquence must shape—to fire and air
To chiming water, the fertile earth, till from it come
Compounded by love, the early trees, the quick
Birds, the intricate
Hidden life of the animals, our human selves
All, all out of the silence—silence of sea or mountain
Flooding back on the riro's dying note or beating
Between the drumbeat of the surf
Like the one personal heart we cannot hear.
                              Unspectacular
Stoic hero, you listened, were not unnerved,
Steady through each ordeal, outstared

Its many faces, horrific or beguiling by turns:
But turning its true one at last, it chose you
And entered your poems:
                              Humbly, deftly woven
Strong nets of silence, they teach us how to listen
Till from them come
Person, place or thing, beast and flower,
The elements, the populated land
And under all, the silence—
                              Like temples
Through their slim
Ionic pillars, their delicate
Arches permitting us their partial
—How else could we see it, or you?—glimpse of the ocean
    beyond.

[MS-2674/143, variant MS-2674/108]

from THE WIND AT RIMINI

  1 Her Room

Though your things in this room are there to appease the eye
With soft surfaces of wood left unpainted
And one picture, a girl reading a letter, her dismay
Evident to us (but how anguish comes transmuted!)

We turn to the window first: a garden steps down in green
Where the narrow inlet tucks its white craft
Far from the sea. A stray gull flashes there
As, in your calm eyes, sudden desolate knowledge.

The room looks west: each day it gathers the dying sun
Into every corner with the sweetness of honey;
And if a wind rise after, will ask no privacy
Facing by choice that quarter where storms come.

2 Her Dreams

I am a country, she says—here are my mountains
Here my gulfs, my long brown promontories.
Or else a piece of luggage, standing forgotten
On a cold platform; or perhaps a curtain
That billows and flaps in a wind blowing from the sea.

In all of which she appears to offer herself:
Bring home your ships, great captain, to my bays
Let them nod forever to the strong pull of my tide.
Carry me with you on your famous explorations
To wrap yourself, at the end, in my wine dark folds.

Dreams prophesy by contraries: the land forever
Remains unknown; the trunk unclaimed.
The curtain flaps and billows at the head of an empty staircase.

Only one dream do we share: each searching the other
Through rooms and corridors, down staircases
Where no-one mounts; and so, till death transform us
To objects—trunks, curtains, earth that suffers anything.

3 *Cosi vidi venir, traendo guai, ombre portate dalla detta briga*

Wind came that day, darkening the sea's blue
To cyanide, and clashed together the fishing boats
At their moorings near the café where we ate.

Gulls drew
Their lament over the cliffs, lost to our view
In the murderous sea that toiled at the cliff's foot.
The day was cold, snow had suddenly come
To mountains in the west, after the prolonged
Advance of autumn that wore us down with hope.
You warned me August would be cold. You knew
Now what you meant. The wind stung
Tears from our eyes, roughened our lips and hands:
Even our grief was dry. Loss
Flashed a curved wing between us, till the ban
Grew legible in our features, where we read no more.
The sea's jaws leapt
To the wedding ring I hurled: they suck it thin.

The engines of your plane roared overhead
You lay above me with a coat of snow
Fear ground our loins together, we were dead

Till the wind pried us apart again, and blew
Us down the long brown street: we were swept
Into our twilight room, our voices rustling hoarse.
We waited there for night, and neither wept.

   4 Last Night

If you could tell the dawn was coming
It was because the hills took on a deeper black
Brooding more stubbornly over the shifting waters.

You would not say these two could ever part:
Such joy and pain brought them together that night.

All the way there, one wild chant ran in his head
Guiding his hands and feet beyond his knowing.

All the evening she waited, hoping, not hoping
But lifting her eyes to attend to a wild chant

And when they met, it was like two waves meeting
Whose ripples penetrate the remotest corners of night;

And woke thereafter to find each other again
Their wordless cries of terror or love
Stitching hour to hour of night in joy and pain.

Why then, when night was done, did he rise and leave?
Why did she leave, shutting the windows, smoothing the bed

Leaving, both of them leaving, the house like an empty shell
To listen to the tides of day and night roar overhead?

All night they could tell the dawn was coming
All night the hills took on deeper and deeper black.

5

I drove past your house last night:
The blinds were down, all the doors were shut;
On the path we weeded, all the weeds had grown up again.

Green light still held the hills opposite
But the sun was gone, there was no gold on the window.
The house watched me as the dead watch: still, without seeing.

It was as though someone had closed your staring eyes
Not out of pity, but with a desire for tidiness
And had gone away then, swinging the keys.

[*Landfall* Volume 19 Number 2 June 1965, variant MS-2674/143]

ELEGY TO MAECENAS

In the end, they bring what one wants, the lean obsequious years
My servants now: it's a young man's way
To rail at their depredations. I did myself
Lamenting youth, with not one hair turned grey.

Come, old friend. Leave your affairs for once.
Ambassadors can wait. I've had a meal prepared
For a long time now: light mountain wine to suit
Our infirmities: there's perfume for your hair
A little music, a pretty child to play.
All's done, as it should be done. We'll talk of books
Politics, old scandals, what you will:
Two greyheads in the tolerant sun.
I've no need to praise
Surely, your achievements? There they lie
File upon file thick with honourable dust.
Rome shrinks with all her battles by.
Your city and mine. Statesmen, literary men—
When the cool mind's divorced
From civil act and passion, who can endure
Five minutes' conversation with it? Yet they read
My poems still, those civil monuments
Chiselled from chaos and my catholic lust.
Therefore, when I am dead
They will remember the black hair parting above the brow
Of mad Cinara who once for a whole year
Burned her hot summer in my aching head
Till in the end
I turned her to ash and art.

                    I survive,
Maecenas: so cleverly I lost
All to the wreck of youth, but this clear tongue for wine—
I see your smile. Even that need to boast
Noted in others sourly, ripened at last
To an old man's foible, hangs sweet upon the bough.
All is distinct and calculable gain.
                              The shadow of the day
Grows long. The sea lies still
In the bowl of the sky, still as the wine in your cup
That stands there at your elbow, and you have not touched.
                     Strange, how the eye will stray
From the flute girl's plump and candid thigh
To the enduring curve of the long Calabrian bay.
And further still? Two frosted pinnacles
Half lose themselves in the insubstantial sky …

[1965, MS-2674/143, variant MS-2674/104]

KALLIMACHOS OF KYRENE

I don't like the poems that everyone reads, the load
Of average humanity on an average road;
Or baby who gets around too much—I
Never touch the local water supply.
Come here my honey, come and kiss me quick:
Public property of all kinds makes me sick
And you're an exception—so douce, so steady
What's that the echo said? Gone already?

[1965, *Otago University Review 1888–1971*]

REQUEST FOR A BIRTHDAY POEM

Dear Bridie: entering upon
A warm November night
Sixteen years ago
A small but of course
Untidy
Bird, you screamed your first
Demand, which I
Heard as the demand of Spring
Who fills, on every hand,
Trees with pink ice-cream
In brandy balloons, until
They overflow and spatter
The warm asphalt on
Trim *Highgate*, where I ran
Coatless down *Maori Hill*.
Since that night, neither
You nor she have learned
Respect for age at all,
And its cautious weather,
Nor stopped demanding, and
I hope you never will
For both of us, sweet
Novel thoughts to fill
Transparent forms, and leave
Always
Something we can scatter.

[1966, MS-2674/143, variant MS-2674/104]

'NO FOG: MERELY A THICKENING OF AIR'

No fog: merely a thickening of air
Will confine the discriminate stars
Till they retire from night.
There are no qualities. Trees
Stiffen themselves to endure
An agony of mass and weight
Their leaves hang down
And make no sound.
No-one sleeps in this night.
No-one lives in this town.

The milkman clatters at the gate.

[MS-2674/104]

'ADJECTIVES—SOMETHING THROWN IN FOR GOOD MEASURE'

Adjectives—something thrown in for good measure
And how shall we live without measure, without
Goodness? The handshake which is golden, the smile
So unnecessary, what would we do
Without such luxuries (additive)

Grammarians, disciplinarians (keep in step
Keep your eyes to the front and always remember
The object of the exercise: when found
Neutralise: if possible destroy)
Describe adjectives in puritanical terms:

Something added, something imposed: *ornamented*
(Or a regrettable fashion of saying what things are not).
One ends with a net where the golden
Fish escape through the smallest mesh.

Yet sometimes in the night (and always by accident)
Not working anywhere, nor looking for anything
One comes upon a forest clearing, a moonlit god
Faceless, but catching a shadow

And the tongue stumbles upon a name
Not to be spoken aloud, and the hard
Light silently as a moth upon
A noun both common and proper, without gender
Requiring no adjective.

[MS-2674/104]

FROM A POINT OF VIEW

Another person, say, is a context: an attitude
Or situation, to know which is simply
The power to predict or anyhow
To act. I put the jug down
                    And you pick it up.
Or not. So. The jug at least's true
And would sing to us if it could.
                    But no.

Say then, a garden or greenwood through
Which we wander at will and come
Clear eyed into the sun at last. Or spend our days
Lost in a green afternoon.

                    But see, another moves
From tree to tree, keeps slow pace to make
All prospects the same. From a point of view
One sees only a view.
                    And you?

[MS-2674/104]

MATUTINAL

The sun's fireball, suddenly released
Jerks up from the horizon. Every blade of grass,
Every stone, touched with peculiar truth.
The surf neighs like a horse
And gallops landward with row on row of bared teeth.

Bright day of sacrifice! Still asleep
I sway like an anchored lily in the light
Fluid around me. My dreams grip deep
To bedrock in your darkness and oppose
The cold influx, the long slide into life.

Each stone and grass blade in the morning light
Casts a distinct shadow. Over the bare
Cloven hills the short-lived birds declare
Their territory. The huge day expands
Its wedge between us, and our eyes come clear.

Day severs us. I wake to my birthright
Among the grey tents of Israel, dispossessed
Of warmth and darkness. I wake to feel
Light's thumb against my throat, and in my hand

Some broken, useless weapon. I am free,
Cold as a stone. Our hands search, for a warmth
Lost under the world's rim, and cannot meet.
But the sun shines, the hills are there!
                              Sheathed within
Me I carry daylight like a sword.
Stiff-backed I ride the naked hills alone.

[MS-2674/143, variant MS-2674/104]

AT PEARL BAY

The sea was calm that day, the sky clear.
The sea moved, however: one would say it breathed
Like a child sleeping, like a woman after love.

Its fingers fluttered along the ledge, moved up and down;
Explored, as if in dream, the remembered land;
Reassured itself, and sighed: the land became its dream,

The cloudless sky, the summer afternoon, itself
Till in its sphere, a second dream took form
Another land, another summer, and back, and back

Till afternoon was locked in afternoon
Summer within summer, yet each more like the first—
Endless repetition!

But see! on the horizon, the furthest point of light
Last meeting place of form and colour, a unique sail
Scooped in minuscule, faint sliver of air

Blue transparence of bone china, holding its course
All afternoon between the sky and sea
Steers toward loss forever, and cannot drown.

[1966, MS-2674/143, variant MS-2674/104]

CUNNING ODYSSEUS

Cunning Odysseus, cunning Penelope
He, led home by cunning
To the bed kept warm by cunning

Like any old beggarman, his cap
Over his eyes, greasy collar turned up
Cocked an eye through the window before knocking

She, quick to detect a stranger
Under the quite expected disguise
Matched cunning by double cunning:

Nearly domestic, heard by the fireside
A lying tale, the cat's eyes watching
Words creep under their silk

Till across the great bed facing each other
By cunning, by cunning, could they frankly drop
The various disguise that brought them here?

Or in simple cunning, with much to tell
More to conceal, did they work their way
To the closest grip, the most defended?

[1966, *Otago University Review 1888–1971*, variant MS-2674/143]

II ∾ Recreations (1967, 1970)

To the Disposer

PART ONE

1

Shop windows turn their light upon the street
The world is outside in, and in my hand
A crumpled ticket is a candle end
The cold wind blows it out around my feet.

The window dresser's room shines back: not dress
But Platonic Form of dress; the sequins shine
Upon her skirt, I am at light's confine,
What candle lights me from the mind's distress?

The dummy's hand moves through benevolent air
In stillness; the cigarette eternally burns
And youth is unconsumed; the dancer turns
Remaining still; purples and yellows glare.

They glare like truth; the world is outside in,
I am in dark, the world of light is here
The painted lips form words I cannot hear
And time is absolute, and stands between.

2

It may happen at any time, for any cause: your pen
Falters and stops at the misspelt word; perhaps
On the table your eye falls on a haphazard stain
Among the cups, and the talk and the clattering cups

Fade past the thundering curtains of despair;
And as though behind a wall of glass, lips frame
Their unechoing words in that remote world where
You no longer are. And everything is the same

As beneath you at an indivisible point
So under you feet you cannot bend to see
The broad earth drops away, and at a point
In the eye's corner, from the darkening sky—

And everything is the same. Such the talk, the table, such.
Love is the word you hear, the wood you touch.

3

On the sand hill, lupin blooms
And flickers along the sky like fires
The seeds explode, sharp as words
On the vague air's

Simulacrum of warmth and light.
In pools collected shadows lie.
Only the bursting lupin speaks
Out of its mindless haste to die.

Your still head before me looms
The one real object in the sky.
The dying sun salutes with fire
Your lips that speechless signify.

The word intangible consumes
A world where suns and flowers die
Passing to shadow. You, standing there
Mount like a flame towards the sky.

4

The dress you wear
Holds in its narrow prison all my care.
I walk in you
From soft crown to pointed shoe.
Not here but there I
Am near as breast or thigh
And nearer than you're aware.

Strange, to be
So at one with you, though recently
Lips and thighs
Parted in glad franchise
Or freed from their modish fear
Those breasts lay bare
And I was not there, but here.

5

Some women, they say, in your circumstances
Have taken to knife or noose or phial
Loading an astonished stage with corpses

A text with splendid morals. Not so with you:
Indifference, lacking hands or eloquence
Affords no spectacle, no soliloquy.

No metamorphosis can give wings to what
In the long nights, dumb as a moth destroys
Love neglected in the heart's locked cupboards.

6 Orpheus to Eurydice

How are the shops in Hades—are they good?
Do you pick up something new, that no-one there
Has thought of wearing yet—some absurd hood
Or long mauve cloak, that only you could wear?

There'll be poets too, no doubt—I don't suppose
I was the first, in spite of what they say;
And if I charmed by love or speech, who knows
What forgotten tongues, what ancient skills, might play
Five senses into modes we never guessed?

7

Now he has gone, in petulance or boredom,
Leaving a shirt thrown across the bed,
Studs on the dressing table, perhaps a coathanger—

Now you no longer hear him, blundering
About the room at 3 a.m. or wake to feel him
Humped oblivious at your back

You carefully tidy, I know, these reminiscences
Into some convenient drawer, humming quietly
And plan to redecorate a room;

While he elsewhere grows sentimental in the evening
With glass in hand, and formulates your despair—
Let him not pity you, or himself:

What fresh outrage of desertion can impinge
On your serene mind, its knowledge of death,
Its passion for tidiness?

8

When the act we would
Parodies our dreaming
All may be understood
By a willing make-believer;
And so forgive, he said
My hands for their presuming
And quietly she smiled
And her eyes said never.

And after, he spoke again:
Where is the light that left me
Alone on a featureless plain
Where night around grew denser?
Outside, the indifferent rain
Fell in the garden softly
Where a shy, blundering hedgehog
Paused to await her answer.

There was no sound outside
But the tree's weeping;
Still she had not replied
The night could pause no longer
Till a wrathful bird cried
Her from his anxious keeping:
In anger, in despair
She took him like a stranger.

9

Between the time of you and I
There was time
To close an eye

Between the flight from lip to ear
There was still time
Nothing to hear

Between the meeting of breath with breath
Blank miles of time
And frozen death.

Time for two parrots to glide
From nowhere and nowhere, flush
With colour the tree outside

And bob, and be gone elsewhere:
How shall we know, ever
Such vivid birds as were there?

PART TWO

    10

One may grow angry with it: it is like a person
Like living in a person, having one's blood
Run through channels of his decision, the head

Twitching with his. To awake in the sour
Distillation of another's nightmare is panic;
No longer to know the back of one's hand, an affront.

It directs your loving: before you are aware
It will step from the crowds beside you and insolently
Salute your darling. Its kiss

Will breed no fruit; it has tenderness
But not to water the areas of mistrust:
Different, the object of its careful erosion.

Its time is the snake's or the nervous lizard's, an antique time
Set to the listening desert, where the cracked earth
Turns from the sun, and the sun pursues it without love.

Its accretion of life is not innocent: only the tree is innocent
Leaping moonward, or the waterfall
Crumbling the granite with patient love.

11

All that night, and through the next and through the next
Thick surf foaming about me thumped
My head on rock on sand
                          The curious fish unsexed
My loins, waves lifted me and dumped

My sodden parcel of flesh. Nails fell from my hand
That groped in shingle, and the long green lash
Knotted about my ribs and then unwound
My rolling body to the slow backwash.

I was the sea's, the wind's, who had set my skill
Against their strength, I who had known
The equipose of tide with gale, defined
As Palinurus to the viewless wind
And the unaltering star I sailed for, till
The just elements claimed me for their own.

12

Still ignorant of his power, he essayed
In terror of ignorance still higher flight
And trod the air with panic.
                        The air spread
Its hands below with love, and bore his light

Limbs upwards beyond cloud and gull
And the familiar shaped islands, till within
That ultimate region he found his skill
And calmly downward, homeward—

                          The sun

Had kissed his back too hotly: tossed
In the murderous paws of air he became
Flesh, bone, clay, stone, a falling thing
For winds to tear at and the sea to crush

And the vast sky flaunted his tattered wing
And the vast sea syllabled his name.

13

This man perished beyond the speed of sound
Beyond love's encircling whisper, or any cry
Of wonder or lament. The blue whistled about his ears
As the distant earth was turning.

Mad on flying, they said, from boyhood up:
His desire was older than words he framed it in.

Only the trees, the aspiring grass he left below him
Can tell what sent him hurtling

Only the long dead under the grass, they
Whose earth filled eyes are burning.

14

Not the breath of the rabble, acrid with lust now
Not the white face of the torturer, bending over him
Nor the south wind nor the north wind nor any wind
Whipping to greater fury what was always unquiet

Not these—
> nor if at his simple question the bent

World crack suddenly, tumble, can ruin alter
What is now and forever complete in every moment.

As clouds the heroes, the Epicureans, look down with indifference
From the top of the immemorial staircase—their mouths
Are stained with purple, their eyes bulge, they do not
Move, they do not avert their heavy gaze.

With distorted lips, rapt oracles are prophesying
Alteration in heaven, a petulant goddess performs
Her worst upon some city, and history extends
From the last step of the staircase to the first.

15 Electra

My grief's a black hole where my father lies
Under nettle, in a corner by the wall.
Child's play, to keep it from my mother's eyes:
It's pretty now, with green fern, mirror, shell.

Sharp Trojan seas sliced up that modest girl
I've buried in a twist of pinafore.
Watched by old eyes, my blunted fingers spell
Over the worn names on the backhouse door

Till they swarm like insects. At last the day comes cool
Through the palace window and my doll begins
To turn her propped head to the pointing light
Where my long brother rises from the night.

16

Their forefathers, moving through a fluent
World of winds and rivers, forests and streams
Saw life as movement, death as other movement
Lived undisturbed till they observed what forms

The wind made as it brushed the mountain side
And the river as it swirled under the rock:
To such dim permanences of the tide
Gave their own names, and understood their talk
Mating with them. Their sons came from the sea
Blonde demigods fated to die too soon
With something of its salt austerity
Stiff on their brows and lips.
      Sailing alone
The grey wastes of their mind, they understood
Death as no human or immortal could.

17 Death

Is to take one last cool look around the room
At things you used so long: loved, and a burden.
Gently you close the door, you will not disturb them.
Dawdling down the steps, you pocket the keys:
The evening's still: you whistle a fragment of tune
That nobody, now, will hear.
      Suddenly a breeze
Stirs in an unswept corner, reminding you who stood
There last, and what he said, or how he looked.
Then others come, and others: how they press
Into that vacancy, with their ancient claims

Their insistence, their bitterness, their distress
Till love plucks at your sleeve, and again you burn:

They are with you now forever, wherever you turn.

PART THREE

18

To hide one's madness among the mad
Carefully shading the eyes and mouth
As under a large round hat

To hide one's grace among the agile
Out at elbows among the teacups
Treading on the favourite cat

To hide one's eloquence among the eloquent
Beginning the story from the dunce's corner
Losing, half way, the point—

And after to loose grace, eloquence, madness
Like birds against the dumb ribbed sky
And watch them strangely fly.

19

The worst part is the waking dream. Earlier
When cells weary as public rooms have quaked
To silence, and you no longer occupy
Their shrouded chambers
                      Should long mirrors
Reflect a shuffling ghost or gentle clerks
Re-emerge as booted interrogators, you are unaware of it
And perhaps they don't.

Later, you discover
You had slept too well; the fishing was too perfect
The affair too out of this world. Your body
Turns to its dreadful task of self-creation
And this time without help: legs, unwieldy
As tree trunks must be found and willed through
Sinking distances, and painfully fitted. Hands flap
Inarticulate at sad infinities; you know the panic
Of nausea, and no apparatus to be sick with.
Finally there is the breathless search for the head
Which a scatter-brained body has always
Managed to mislay, and at the last minute:
'Supposing, this time
I wake without one?'—beside which elementary panic
That memories should be settled like distracted birds
Into an accustomed identity seems mere detail.
Somehow it all happens, and here is the day
Sliding familiarly over the sill. Outside
Are the noises of summer, and the sun benevolently presiding
Over the major recreations.

20

Leaves fall, leaves fall
Some yellow, some that sudden autumn froze
Their green not marred at all.

Skies change, skies change
Winds tear their sullen blanket to disclose
Stars clear beyond our range.

Love stays, love stays
To bind us in a pattern that we chose.
Loosen the string, scatter the withered days.

21

She is young, young as the green grape
Her breasts are hard, hard as the green grape
Unyielding is her waist
Yet should you taste
Her love is bitter as the green grape.

A ripe grape bursting on your tongue
Grape swallower, makes you and the day one
In sweetness, and the savour past
You are yourself at last
And spread, vine wise, in the sun.

Taste her, bite her—she'll sting you
Till you are soured to nothing
But a green sigh curled
Round her unbroken world
Whose bitterness all tastes now bring.

22

Lift your head, stag, lift your antlered head.
On plains below the sunless rivers spread.
The cold sun sinks. The cold cliff holds its red.

There are no men and women here, to sing and dance
There are no gods here, to sing and dance.
Your antlers show the earth's exuberance.

No antique horn rang here, no hound's bay:
You turn away, as the cold cliff turns away,
As the cold earth turns, from the sun. Stay.

23

After years, he learned to welcome the summer:
Despair a condition of existence, like the sun
Which excused the sluggish insolence of shopkeepers
And the hostile stares settling on him like flies.

Or when the barbaric wind swept from the North
Freezing wine, turning dust into slush
He was glad that fire and warmth were unquestionable values
That all places alike seemed mud.

Spring of course was the season most unendurable:
The sour creek becoming an illusory river
And the wind blowing off water somewhere
And the tossing willow a slim girl half dressed

And the sailing season begun, and blossom hung highways opened
To the brilliant capitals of the South
(appeals, representations, painstakingly composed
and never reaching any destination)

—Even the spring no longer vexed him: he rejoiced
At the boughs struggling into blossom, the impertinent
Lovers—writing poetry again, pottering
At odd jobs, growing vegetables, acknowledging death.

24

In the spring and autumn, mice invade my house.
They come from the field, from the tall grass where they belong
And slide along drainpipes, tumble down chimneys, walk impudent
Over the sunlit doorsill where I read my paper.

They set up their miserable homes in the corners of cupboards,
Under the bath, behind the fireplace. They leave traces
In dark places for me to put my hand on. They appear
In my breakfast and dinner, and in the evening
They poke out their clever faces from the shadows.
At night, I lie awake
And listen, conscious, for the first to begin.
It seems the whole world is not room enough for us both
And I do not think I could bear it, but there is always the thought

That next month or next year I will find another house:
A new house, still smelling of paint and plaster
With no food in it, nothing damp or dirty or rotten,
Nothing to attract a mouse. Or perhaps one so old
That everything in it has perished or been devoured
Where the small multitude has come and run riot
Held its Bacchanalia, and left no regret.

25

The children across the road were undesirable.
Their house lacked paint, the door leaned from its hinges
Besides, the plumbing was inadequate

Which perhaps explained (though not excused) the foulness
Of their knees or nails or noses.
      Under their matted hair

Their eyes flashed with austere beauty; the secrets
They disclosed under the shrubbery startled
The mimosa into sudden blossom and filled the air
With loud, protesting, song.

26

Grace in this landscape is hard to find. If you rise
Beyond six you may not, when the sun is already
High over the cirque of hills, and the flies
Repossess the scented air and under the steady
Thud of the heat roads vibrate through their haze.

Taking your axe in your hand, you slowly turn
To the woodheap, thinking elsewhere perhaps, but never
Raising your head to where the low hills burn.
Chips fly at you, the thick red dust lodges
Malignly in your nostrils, and what you earn

Is immediately apparent in the growing heap.
Or pressing your head in the cow's flank, while she flicks
Her tail at the flies, you watch white bubbles leap
Up the filling pail, and grimly count what it takes
To make average gain. The sun will gradually creep

To its rainless zenith. In town, you gaze
At the stockman's calendar, which glossily depicts
The fortunate idle by white falls of surf, till seas
Stun you like music. Too soon their sound contracts
To the ticking clock, and the flies, the flies.

Outside in the street, a fat fox terrier sprawls
On the baking asphalt, and the bored aboes wait
On seats outside the courthouse, where an average fate
Is averagely debated. The sparse shadow crawls
Back under its tree to emerge, unwillingly, late

In the afternoon. Then, unschooled children go
Indian file along the creek bed, whose scored
Sands hold a memory of water. They know

How to fantasy aridness may afford
Under the parching stars a nightlong flow

Of water, grace. Here: and in the lovers' room
Where the amorous candle dies in the varied dawn
And in four corners kindly the shadows loom
While through the window green tides of air are borne
Flieless as yet, faintly scented with gum.

27

We who never cared for gardens
Journeying to places where we could unfurl
Simply as a map some fluid prospects
Of plain, forest, river, hill
And watch them to a reminiscence harden

Enclosed at last our vision in this plot
—Four wooden fences and a gate—and move
Along the rows now, hoe in hand, to check
What chokes in idleness the roots of love—
Diligent in our small service we forgot

How landscapes turn to desert. Which of us now
Would not weep at the splintered trees, the dry
Watercourses, the stones, the dust? or choose
That journey ending in a sigh
Where death has lost its greenness?
                                              But to allow

The gate to click behind and tall weeds grow,
Bent on another journey, where all's unsure
No map or memory, no way to lose?
Strange that I hesitate so long before
The gate, or swing it idly to and fro.

III ∞ Living for Others

Fragmentary poet, pray for us poets who
Live by fits and starts, living for others
In others, never ourselves, never at home:
Scribblers, scribbled on by time
Ripped out by time, discarded for ever
Fragments of our world, who begin with fragments—
Pray for us, that our limitation
May give our lives much sense.

—'You Died at Nineteen'

'THE SNOW MELTS QUICKLY FROM THE HILLS'

The snow melts quickly from the hills.
Within an hour
I have watched the grey hillside creep through again
Like scarred time
From an avoidable accident.

Last night the hedges were brimming like cups
As though all summer they had been growing
Just for this: to have their black skeletons
Filled with blossoming snow.

The trouble is, it is not snow country,
Not properly: too far north or south
It fails, a dilettante of the ascetic
And of the voluptuous, a little of both.
Yesterday, snow. Tomorrow, a day
Of extraordinary mildness.

But today it thaws. Patches
Of grey or black grow wider, streets
Reappear, the water runs down
Between houses, and life goes on
But aware of imperfection.

[MS-2674/104]

'I DO NOT CLAIM'

                  I do not claim
Difference from other men—only aware
Of the world when it presents itself
In its crudest form: as if I stood

Awkward, hat in hand, trying not to stare
As the sunlight wakes your thighs
                          —Or as the new born child
Gropes instinctively towards
The warmth that is no longer
His own warmth.

[MS-2674/104]

from 'I THINK OF YOU'

Your word sometimes seems
A net of such silence: slim pillars, perfect
Arches that allow us
To glimpse the ocean beyond.

[MS-2674/104]

'WHY DO YOU PUT UP WITH ME?'

Why do you put up with me?
I ask you. Even one's best friends
Are not told some things
They are, we say, ignoble:
But they are worse than ignoble—
We pretend to ignore them as
Aristocrats aiming at
A certain stillness of feature
Pretend to ignore their serfs
In their repetitive, menial tasks.
Neither serf nor noble we aim
At stillness and cannot be still.

And men must share their lives—
Though all they require is distinction—
At any price: this gentle
Wave-like movement, this slow
Abrasion of joint, this confusion
Of swamp life. Nothing
Is what it was, nothing
Can be distinguished.

It wears us down.
It blunts the sharp edges which
We found to correspond
To our delight.
Over a distance
We saluted each other
According to the fine convention
Of an archaic code.
Do you think that now
You could find me in a crowd?

Why is no man an island?
I think of you as an island—
Small, no more than a rock, half
Hidden by waves that surround it, and
Out of sight of any land
That a rare sea bird
Visits sometimes—
Always the same place.

Yes, or as that mare
We once observed: flicking
Her tail as we paused, she gently
Turned and walked quietly away

From the road and up
To the trees where a clear
Stream issued: purposefully, as if to some
Destination beyond
Our coarse imaginings.

[MS-2674/104]

'IF IN THE MORNING'

If in the morning
I get up, leaving
The long cool unbroken
Stain of your body in
The bed where I have trampled
All night like a wild
Stallion trapped in a paddock
And
Looking down
At you looking
Up at me
Tenderly, tell you
That love is
Shit

Well
That too
Is a tribute.

[MS-2674/104]

TRADITIO

I had invited you to my private feast
To share the still untorn bread, the single cup
The common taste of salt—

You could hardly refuse. Yet time deals
The pack so crudely. When you came
Puzzled, shy, we had been strange for centuries.

Now nightly your eyes explore the ceiling
And the wine spreads between us on the board.
Yet hatred could not be so clumsy:

A third, seeing our two heads bent here
Might recognise in a flash the common archetype
Placing us father and son.

[*Landfall* Volume 21 Number 2 June 1967, AS]

GLACIER

Do not go too near
The glacier's face:
                though suspended
In a permanent snarl that seems
Ossified it is not
Dead: the huge river escaping
From underneath with a panic
Yell can tell you
That.
    But having
Shot out its paw once
In a time so long ago
That there was nothing

Around to measure the speed
Of its defining gesture
It now
Draws it back lazily, inch
By year, still rolling
Twenty-foot boulders like peas
And a river runs where it scratched:
Wild, with rearing
Waves, heedless
In its terror of the tangled
Bush on either side
Rooted and growing
Among tumbled boulders
Or of ourselves, tourists
Who struggle with patience
Along a narrow path against
The river's course, resisting
Its Bacchic
Invitation to join in, cast
Our bones to the flood and speed
Of resolved ice.
                    Struggling
Upstream, guided
To where the glacier begins
Or ends, with the inviting
Roar in our ears it seems
We will never
Make it. At last
We come there, where the trees
Finish and the rootless
Shale clatters and the grey
Face hangs.

All superlatives
Are equal in any
Language where tourists
Pick bravely among the detritus
Of a creative era:
The glacier
Limits our journey and
Nothing can express it, but lying
In bed in another year
I wake and within me I hear
The loud river run, the bones tumbling.

[AS, variant MS-2674/104, fragment MS-2674/143]

SHORT STORY

Kostas and I sat
By the ship's rail—I am not sure now
If that was his name, but he had a son
Back in Cyprus who played
Football, professionally, and had not seen
His father for several years. The wife
Does not write. Kostas and I
Sit by the ship's rail drinking
Turkish coffee and watch
The Indonesian islands float by.
The morning sun ricochets
From the steely surface of the sea
Upwards into our eyes. His are old,
Mine young; for different reasons
The light hurts them
Making us both sleepy.

He shows a photograph of his son:
I ask him the name of things
Our eyes half closed against the light.

The young man, black-moustached, grave
Rests his hand on the photographer's table
And might be his own grandfather.
Mumming gently
The ship sails northward
Through the Indonesian sea
Whispering of the past and the future.
'Is called
Thalassa'—indicating the sea
With a broad gesture as though
He gave it to me at that moment.
The name is new, the sea a deeper blue
Than I have seen it.

We talk softly, above the sea's
Sparkle: it is hot, zesto.
Australia too is hot. Australians
Drink much beer, but in Cyprus
They drink wine: his father
Once owned a vineyard there
Near Limassol, where he was born.
In Sydney he worked
First in a timber yard, two
Years, then on the railways
Five years, cleaning
Carriages. His landlady
A kind woman, also
Drinks much beer: at Singapore
He expects a letter. Perhaps I will help him

With the answer: his English
Is not good. He seemed a simple man
And talked, too, of his son
Who must now enter the army—
Watching a sea bird
Perch briefly on the ship's stern—
'Laros.'
   The green
Glittering islands through which we sail
Appear paradisal, uninhabited.
I repeat the name 'nesis, nesia'
Sleepily, like a child.

As the sun climbs to noon
Far off, blue through the distance, a mountain
Pierces the morning sky—
'Vouno, vouno,' pointing
With his gnarled hand.
'In my country, there are many vouna'

The bright morning closed
Over our heads again.
I remember his name now, Iannis.

[October–December 1967, MS-2674/108, variant MS-2674/104, MS-2674/143]

'WE RETURN FROM A WALK TOGETHER'

1

We return from a walk together: the blood jabs
Under our skin drawn taut with the cold.

It leaps and it drums like a small impatient goblin.
It whines and it frisks
It sits up and it begs
Then it lies down and simply roars—
Begging to be let out.
What mischief it would make, what confusion
Of things not to be confused!
But we are hard, practical,
And won't let it out.
I build a fire and light it, you
Put the child to bed.
These evenings are not to be wasted!

   2

There is a clear
Shape, a defined volume, an apple
Hard and round and ripened by frost—
Something to hold in the hand. I did not
Think I would know it again: the worm in my mind
Had bitten so deep, so deep he lay
Alone curled and showed
No sign of moving. The whole world
Had dissolved in his abrasion: soft, brown,
No thing had its taste or substance, only the bitter
Worm, like a rusted nail upon the tongue
Or a nail through the heart—
Nail or worm, small curled worm
How could you cure it?
                         See,
The whole apple lies open now
And there is no worm: at the crisp centre

Only the seeds, shiny and hard with promise.
And there is peace, whole days
Of hard effort rounded with autumn firelight
And long walks in the evenings, hand in hand
Or in single file along narrow paths, treading
The soft brown leaves where branches hang
Sharp against the green sky, sharp as that star—
Talking or not talking, the man, the woman, the child
Silent and distinct as strangers first met:
Intimate, as if we had grown
Three in one from some solid block of stone.

[MS-2674/104]

THE GREEN BIRD

Even to see is hard enough:
       All
The varieties of green leaf
Hidden among so many leaves
That they seem one
And the bird lost among them
That is not a leaf:
       And the light so short
Stabbing between these clouds:
         Bright.
Dark. Bright. And again
Bright.
  But breaking up
Or finally gathering, how can one tell?
The bright or dark

Moment can tell
One nothing.
         Deeper
In the green wood the green bird calls.

[MS-2674/104]

'YOU DIED AT NINETEEN'

You died at nineteen. You never married
Though old enough to know what it meant.
Childhood, estrangements, death—you lived it all
In the death of your friend, more truthfully
Than anyone could have said.

The rough edge of chance
Stopped the delicate beat of your years
Tearing the next line through. Scholars count and surmise
And cannot tell us our loss—yet who
Could reckon yours, supposing that you
Or the papyrus had lived? Suppose for once
That time and chance knew better?

Fragmentary poet, pray for us poets who
Live by fits and starts, living for others
In others, never ourselves, never at home:
Scribblers, scribbled on by time
Ripped out by time, discarded for ever
Fragments of our world, who begin with fragments—
Pray for us, that our limitation
May give our lives much sense.

[MS-2674/104]

'UNACCOMPANIED BY DOG OR MEMORY'

1

Unaccompanied by dog or memory
I walk the vacant golf-course above the city
And am my own. I come from nowhere
And go nowhere: I have no home
Walk now fast now slow, retrace my steps counting
Or wait, under a silent tree
I think nothing, remember nothing
For an hour, this way, am free.

2

This only, that way—what few chances
For love or music I may have mined.
Still, to be free is something—and why
Always put oneself in the way of it?
See, the evening's empty, still—it stays
Because it has nowhere to go, nothing to say.
The tree is simply a tree. It sleeps.
Like children or like dogs
One's desires grow bored at last and wander away.

3

Maybe a poem is like that: a child
Waiting too long for a word that no-one
Remembered to say, until no longer a child
Slipped without comprehension into one grey
Unforgiving world of its own—unforgiveable
Simply to love a thing that way.

4

A last gleam
Clings to a funnel in the harbour
The night wind
Rises: suddenly the evening's gone
The sky filled with stars
How many of us are there!
The wind blows, the leaves are turning
Night fills us, night makes us one

[MS-2674/104]

DEE WHY MORNING

In Billings' timber
                yard (Special
Discounts for the Home-
builder) where Pete the Dutchman
works a light
European frost still clings
to the rough end of some things
but don't
worry it will soon disappear
in the dry Australian sun
while his tomorrow
                waits
under a faded Woolworth frock

[MS-2679/104]

EPITAPH

Weathereye—
         hand—
                  tiller—
the whole
harpstrung
tense
    harmony the crest
lifts high
the racing seas
outrun.

[MS-2674/104]

ERINNA'S LAMENT FOR BAUKIS

    (after *The Distaff*)

Mad girl, from the white horse's back
Straight into the wave you
Jumped! 'Tag!' I would shout 'I've
Got you!' Darling
You were already more than halfway
Across the long playground.

The ground is still warm where
You set your feet. Kids' games—
Ash.

Oh, the Bogeyman!
When we were girls
We slept side by side
Not a care in the world
Clinging to our dolls—
Brides.
        And in the dawn
        Your mother came to wake you.

Oh, the Bogeyman!
With four feet
And long, long ears!
Now see his face.
Watch it.
Watch it changing.

When you married
You could not remember
A thing your mother taught you:
Little girl
In the bed of a man
You could not
Remember.

Aphrodite laid forgetfulness
Between us.

Therefore
I lament for you
Baukis but
My feet
May not leave the house
My eyes

May not look on you dead
My hair
Be uncovered.
For shame
I may not cry
Where men can hear.

[July 1968, MS-2674/143, variant MS-2674/104, MS-3737/164]

UGOLINO AND HIS SONS

> *Padre mio, ché non m'aiuti?'*
> —*Inferno*, XXXIII:69

My grin a rictus splitting from ear to ear
I drive with half a mind. I pretend to hear
Your sweet inconsequent prattle, that I cannot bear.

I'm tired, you're tired. It's late:
Our neighbour breaking bottles at the gate
Supper cleared, TV finished for the night—
Time to drive you both home. You climb into the car
Silent: you do not like it, but the way things are
Is a stale phrase with us. Sometimes I catch your stare
In the driving mirror, seeing in my own face
How things are the same, no change there. We race
Through the tangle of the streets like wolves:
Time's tooth is in our flanks, it won't let go,
Whatever. These are streets I know
So well that I can lead you home blindfold.
For a year now, we've come this way:
Our recurrent journey, looping day to day
Covers our bare walls with its tapestry.

Sleep aches behind my eyes; my face, released
To the half dark of the car is creased
Like a rescued scrap of paper. Turned
Away from you, it silently transcribes
Like some gadget in your spy films, the tough jibes
Of your small stoic minds, at a world that robs
Has robbed, will rob you of your birthright.
The car lunges through the domestic night:
My driving's deadly, but you're used to it—
And make no comment. You will not permit
Pity of any kind. Pity stays,
Visitant of intolerable, twitching face
At the door locked carefully behind your eyes.
The journey's a short one, but it takes three years
Backward or forward. Now, we are here.
The moon stares at me from behind the house
Where your mother waits. It tears
Its threadbare curtain and it stares and stares.

We stop, with engine running: the pattern runs
Repetitive, ugly, in my mind. My sons
Here's where I relinquish you. Hiding my yawn
I nod goodnight, and back the car
And think what might befall you on the far
Journey between the gate and your front door.
Driving back, I seem to know relief.
The streets are the same. The moon, aloof
Keeps pace with me above the silent roofs.

[MS-2674/143, variant MS-2674/104]

NOTHING TO DO WITH US

Already we are strange:
We drift apart, on some whimsy of the tide
Gear too battered to help

Bad sailing at the start
But nothing to do with us now
Goodbye …

          We mended gardens,
Made flowers grow: but who remembers?
They have nothing to do with us

Nor we with them: we do not care
And it can't be helped, this slow
Disengagement of the tide:

Shared knowledge was a flower, but there's
No earth for it to grow
In any world we know.

[c. 1968, MS-2674/143]

DUNEDIN WEATHER

So warm last night, we lay
Blankets tossed off, ourselves for covering
And found that enough.

What else, then, could we expect
But the ice cold dragon from the South,
Rain slamming on glass all day?

[MS-2674/104]

TWO HOUSES

One should not revisit an old house. I don't care
For the curtains they have hung in my study
(I read Virgil there, in the worn trough of one wild winter)
In the next room, appeased by love, we'd listen quiet
To the surf thud under its blanket of fog.

Then spring, summer. Here was an ancient gate
Where a cow once, curious, bent down her large square nose
To snuff at the small square fist of our grave baby.

And that post is where we chained our intractable dog.
It got off once but returned, with fire rimmed eyes
Ran crab-wise, snarling at us like strangers
And after that, was little good.
                              Oh ghosts, unstable
Inhabit against their will where others keep warmth:
Do they hear, I wonder
A cryptic sigh from the bed, a laugh go round
The side of the house, five fingers drumming on a table?

This other house, though, is picked clean as a rabbit.
I never lived in it: I remember its windless hollow
Where the fog hung, and the wet road dangerous.
Box and bramble enclosed it, and envious macrocarpa—
A bad place to delay.
                Cleared now for sheep:
They crop a neat lawn where wind snaps through its walls
Since the roof was taken for iron. From the road
I can see, through two windows, clear to the cold Pacific.

[MS-2674/104]

IV ∾ Letters from Ephesus (1970)

FROM ACADEMY HILL

The blue air of a Sunday afternoon
Circulates among the ancient
Sandstone columns, golden now
In the late sun.
                      Where are the voices
The hands moving like flowers?
                              Is there
No-one here? Could so many
Lie huddled under dark roofs on which
The sun beats?
                          No, but
The parks are full of unborn children
White among the trees: their sound
Fails to reach me here, and on the unseen
Harbour I picture
Sails like petals, scattering outwards
Forever, lost, lost in the violet evening.
There is no-one here, no-one.
I have almost forgotten
What year it is or century, whether
The empty seats, the brown
Pictures, the dusty
Golden air remark
That you were here once, who are now gone
Or wait for you to enter, and quietly
Take your seat in some distant year
Who are not yet born.

STREET SCENE

Contractors are demolishing
A building on the corner of
Harbour Terrace. Starting
From inside they gradually
Hollow it out like an old
Tooth. There is a skill about it
Which has to be learned against
The warped nail and the corroded
Waste-pipe joint, in all
Old buildings whose parts conjoin
To outface destruction.

But already some outside
Boys have got to work and simply
Smashed two windows in the dairy
Downstairs. Several pieces of broken
Glass lie arranged in fine
Dust on the counter carefully
Like pennies counted out
For fresh loaves and the morning
Bottle of milk and the assorted
Fruit which in the evenings
Flooded the pavement with yellow and orange light.

There are some things
Which should never be seen—
Such as bone. An old couple
Lived in the flat upstairs
Rusted together
Behind the brass pot and the blind.

Now I can see
Their wallpaper and the wall behind it:
It seems they had no secrets.
First fittings are removed, then whole floors.
Bombs do it elsewhere, here the slow pick.

Now the grey façade
Confronts the morning air sharply
Like a head on an old medal.
It has never looked finer—
The roof is off, it is luminous within
And blue sky pours from the windows.

A small crowd gathers
To see a wall tumble like water.
Soon a new building
Will take tenancy of the air.

FOUR SYDNEY PHOTOGRAPHS

1

Half an hour, by the arterial
Busroute will take you dead
To the city centre.
We return at five, bearing
On our jackets the dust
Of old buildings pulverised,
To our homes and wives and the waiting
Children. We eat dust.

2

The new insurance building, providential,
Rears its thirty-four stories out of
The pit, the cavity, rubble
Of leprous sandstone, rusted iron
And splintered shop signs of a fading blue.
Bright as a new filling
Its steel, stone facing, and tinted glass
Shimmer above the harbour
Iridescent like the neck feathers of
The Phoenix, proverbial bird.

3

The Qantas pilot, pivoting
Above the bridge checks his final bearing
Through trembling ether. Fresh from Rome
He rubs a blue chin and dips
For the long easy descent
Home.
Below, the expressways:
Pacific, Warringah, Eastern Suburbs, Kogarah
Where tiny cars
Move with their given instinct
Over the great sea of being
Each diversely to its own carport.

4

In Macquarie Street
On a summer evening
The buildings are brown as old lady's cake.
The specialists have all gone home:

The orthopaedic
The gerontologist.
Under the jacarandas
Stroll secretaries, students
With golden beards
And sunburnt knees.
There are real books in the Public Library
And the grass in the Domain is green.

The summer evening
Holds in its golden globe
The twin towers of St Mary's
Where sins are forgiven.

ACADEMIC ARCHITECTURE

No doubt the architect was pulling our legs:
In one sweep the eye
Gathers three centuries and comes to rest
On a window, Tudor domestic. The effect
Of a practical joke is always to remind us
Of a real predicament: we may laugh or cry
But how are we to live?
The scholar's correct
Hands at work among neat apparatus
Meet contradictions, and fumble.
The stone, however, is local:
Its being-at-handness no fantasy could reject.
Long pages of manuscript, lines or lives garbled
By corruptions, imperfect erasures, defy
And tempt our belief that truth is single:
A clock's there to tell us time flies.

Its absurd tower
We suddenly realise, is Florentine. Here too
In the grey mediaeval valley, the heraldic colour
Of a passion that breaks its own unities:
And sudden arrogance blinds us.

LETTER FROM EPHESUS

In Ephesus they believe in change
Devoutly. One cannot talk
With an Ephesian:

It is like walking
Across a swamp where the stones
Disappear as one sets foot

On them. The Ephesians
Feel it themselves: it gets them
Into deeper contradiction

Which their buildings express:
It is hard to tell
What they are made of

Although their colours are certainly vivid.
Along miles of coastline
Over rocky headlands

And by long swampy beaches
They confront the dignities
Of the ocean

Which looks as if some day
It might choose to flatten them.
This is what every

Good Ephesian half
Hopes for in
His desperate heart.

They make a brave show
In pinks, blues, yellows and
Occasionally

Orange: but you cannot tell
What their walls are made of.
It makes life difficult

Which for Aristotle was easy:
Buildings are built of wood and stone
And this is their material

Which the architect then arranges.
Also they have a purpose
And in this are like ourselves

Or like the beasts—
Inferior only
In that they are artefacts.

In Ephesus, man is an artefact
A Penelope's web
That patiently unravels itself.

My own house, for instance:
I could not tell you
What the walls are made of.

I think it must be
A kind of aery paper
Though proof against fire

Built out over a swamp
In which it would gradually sink
If it waited long enough.

On bright mornings, the swamp
Has its own life, a life
Of coloured birds: they flicker

In and out of the rushes
And red coral trees, pursuing
With happy cries the golden

Green or blue insects which
They then devour. The swamp
Abounds with these insects

Also snakes which on hot days
Appear in the garden
Like visions, to fascinate

Children with the delicate
Pink of their bellies contrasting
With their dull, black

Backs. Obviously
The swamp is a menace
To health: it will have to be

Drained. It is quite easy
To offend nature: she withdraws
For a time, sulking, but

We are mistaken to suppose
That because angry
She is not also deeply

Hurt. Already
In one corner the reclamation
Of her pagan soul has begun

By means of loads
Of municipal ash, plastic
Detergent containers and sodden

Sheets of building material—
Their pinks and blues
Reflected perfectly in

The still, black water which
They are soaking up.
Decaying

Edible matter attracts
Flies: these constitute
A problem for the philosophers.

If we leave windows unscreened
On a hot day, the white
Ceilings designed

To give an effect of coolness
And space
Start quite simply to bubble

With the black round bodies of flies
Until the whole house
Becomes the skull of a beast

Or of a man, sunk to the eyepits
In a forgotten swamp which swarms
With black, carnivorous insects.

Over the swamp, a factory
Geared to the cheap production
Of building materials

Has the squat permanence one sees
In Roman imperial monuments
Or mounded Etruscan tombs.

STUDIES

1

The City Hospital

Is a kind of
Ship, sailing for
The South Pole
With every window blazing.
When you come out
You see her foundering
In green billows of flowering chestnut.

2

On my desk
Again cleared for a desperate
Campaign
Is a bamboo
Paper knife you bought
Of a white shirted
Smiling Indian in
An Aden curio shop
And carried wrapped
In tissue paper through
The Red Sea.

You gave it to me
On a wet cold Christmas
Day in dull Athens.
                        Long travel
Makes us companions still.

3

In this photograph

I observe two details:
The collar of your jersey
From which your neck
Balancing its sphere of head
Springs straight as a water jet
Is so crumpled
That your smile, aiming at high
Irony
Tumbles back into joy.

4 Ibycus

Spring: Ky-
          do-
                nian
Apples are swelling in
Damp orchards of unplucked girls
Under secret
Leaves the vine flower
Grows
       shameless
                lust
Beds in my belly and dreams
Of autumn storms.

5

When Morgan
Was made an example
On Pinchgut they pitched
The gallows
High.
When asked
For his remarks
On the occasion
He observed:
That the only thing
Which seemed worth mentioning
Was the view of the beautiful
Harbour from
His high

Elevation.

Such fastidiousness
Such deliberate avoidance
Sets a high example:
It was not excessive
To devote a lifetime to it.

V ∾ Seeing the Island

In the morning our fingers parted the darkness tenderly
as our ship's prow parted the water of the still bay
—seeing the island for the first time.

—'Memories of Ithaca'

AFTERNOON TEA IN THE EAST

The Wall opens for us
like the cover of a book.

Perhaps that is why
it seems not impertinent
to pry into lives here:
that of Herr Haarig—
an alert reader notices
how his ringed hand moves
like a butterfly among the Meissen cups.
In the carpeted study
his father's books reach the ceiling
and in the eighteenth century prints
no trace remains of a night in Hamburg
arc lights cutting through the fog
behind the railway trucks, the Gestapo waiting
and the long unheard of years in Buchenwald.
There are so many ways of surviving:
honoured heroes, the Old Guard
fallen later into disgrace
may yet bequeath books, porcelain
and in the New Society
a certain standing.
Haarig may read what he likes
and there is always coal for the stove
though outside, the street lamps dim.
Herr Haarig offers me another cup.
It is all so extraordinarily vivid:
these are real people.

The Wall closes, like a book.

[1971, MS-2674/110]

ODE TO WALTER

Pythagoras, all hail
What no mortal could have done
Thou hast: imposed the Limit
Brought into being the One.
Here, streets tidied of people
There, the assemblies inchoate
Not to be spoken of, not named.
Between wire and minefield run
The watchdogs of the State.

[MS-2674/110]

WEST BERLIN: UNORCHESTRATED NOTES

    Inter-
sected by railways
    quartered
by postal districts
    reduced
cunningly to the gridiron logic
   of the fold-out map

TIERGARTEN

Man is still inventive
has tamed for instance the animals

GRUNEWALD

but not himself:
             in the furtive twitch and gesture
of a youth at the zoo-station
the anger is writhing still

under the thud of bombs
that fell too many to seem irregular

Many are the terrors
nothing is more terrible than man
the tireless questioner:

Is it true that in such cases
one million multiplied by one
is still only one?

I really want to know

Does it matter
which colour or shape you choose?

No answer.

Can you remember
a particular colour that mattered
or seemed to matter—
you were five, remember
by the Wannsee
and it was summer.
Later, in another summer
you thought of a particular shape
and a particular voice:
remembering what Plato said, you laughed
and reached out a hand—

Silence.

          Can
you hear me down there
under the shiny pavements
of the Kurfürstendamm

(I hope you can not:
what else is there to hope?)

Question mark.

O in a forgotten eye
a once city

    TIERGARTEN

is glistening.

[22 February 1971, MS-2674/110, variant 69497 MS-0996-003/215]

MEMORIES OF ITHACA

for Liz. Harlow

   1

The wine, the wine!
And our five senses.

In the morning our fingers parted the darkness tenderly
as our ship's prow parted the water of the still bay
—seeing the island for the first time.
You learn to make love like that: not the first time
nor always the second, but at some time, once.

Twice, if you are lucky.

   2

The smells of an island morning:
fish, and coffee brewing.
Outside the café

the old man
with a tanned bald head
and grey hairs showing through his shirt
sipped his coffee
holding the tiny cup delicately
before answering:
'you will find
that on Ithaca, time passes slowly for everyone.'

3

It is hard lying
on a Greek beach
there are too many stones
and between the stones, thistles.
The olive trees give no shade
and there are ants
who do not accept idleness.
But the sea
will take your scratched body and soothe it
dandling it in fathoms of pure glycerine.

4

As if it knew the time
at half past two exactly
the nor'easter sweeps down from a blue sky
turning the blue madonna of the bay
into a white maenad.
Under the bright afternoon
dust gallops through the street
where no-one is about

and all the shutters are closed.
In our whitewashed room
we lie on a bed together
in the green light of closed shutters
hearing the wind roar through the olive trees.
Just think! for thousands of years
it has blown like this.
Its song is not for us:
it is singing to the island
as if there were no continents anywhere.
Just listen!

5

And, taste.

When we awake, the wind has dropped
and already the lights around the bay
few enough to know each other personally
converse across the still, black water.
Sound carries, too: from the restaurant
a juke box whines, pleasantly
as Eliot's mandolin.

The wine of Ithaca is not red:
it is amber.
Also it tastes of honey
and the bitter smoke of fig trees.
It is rough as a donkey's hide.
It may make you drunk
but it will not encourage you to lie.

[MS-2674/110]

COUNTRY WALK WITH GUIDE-BOOK

The barley, rumpled
like the hot fur of the cat
begs the wind: 'Stroke me.'
There is no wind.

'Turning right, to become
a winding country lane …'
Scraps of paper, of body linen
make patent what they enfolded:
left, a regular controlled cry
reaches me from the county asylum.

'Proceed left some 500 yards
along the Welwyn Road'
With manic precision
cars shear at the verges
Grandma riding the back
a bloated image of death.

Thread of my life
what holds you upright?
surely you tremble
in the windless air?

'Many a ripe old
country character …'
Here is her seventeenth century cottage
here her sweetly blooming roses
here come her dogs
here are their teeth.

'From here, a public footpath'

> PRIVATE PROPERTY
> KEEP OFF

'… past the new housing estate …'
Squealing children
watch daddy hose the car.
(The oats beg: blow, wind
the road: fall, rain.)

Later, it rained
with a crack of thunder
fields, trees, blur
tyres on the motorway swish

foxgloves nod when they pass.

[MS-2674/110]

CHANGE OF SEASON ON THE WAY TO THE STATION

What did it remind me of, that wind?
Catching suddenly at that man's tie
and blowing it over his shoulder?
Suddenly it seemed we were a thousand years on
walking down the street, past the blank
shop fronts, Grodzinski's the pastrycook
and the kosher butcher
                        he still ahead of me
I still behind, both of us walking
with broad shoulders, the wind catching at both of us

You were a thousand years away.

It had, I remember, been hot for days:
windless, the trees spreading in the heat
sifting no wind through their fingers
the reservoir's surface a perfect mirror.
For days, the needle had not moved.
We read, I remember, during the days
and at night lay in each other's arms, quietly
the reservoir's surface a pocket mirror.

Suddenly the wind, this drift of light:
he walking in front, I walking behind him
the wind blowing his tie over his shoulder.
It was a thousand years back, or forward.

You were a thousand years away.

[MS-2674/110]

'A CANTEEN IS PROVIDED'

A canteen is provided
for sole use by employees
(regular) or such occasional visitors
as may have received permission
to use this and other facilities.
Dogs would not be welcome
nor for that matter baboons:
smoking of course is permitted.
Men and women eat together
sometimes at the same table
toilets however are separate
men's on the ground floor
and women above.

This separation on the vertical axis
permits conjunction on the horizontal
not because the natural product of digestion
is more offensive than its cultural counterpart
especially when the cooking is English
the processes too are complementary:
they even provide paper table napkins.
With some detachment
I observe my fellow ingestors
male and female
and refrain from describing their behaviour.
It is only later I realise
(in the ground floor washroom)
that a long filament of spaghetti
has for some time adhered
to my beard.

[MS-2674/110]

DEATH OF A CULTURE

Do not misunderstand me: I too comprehend
the new moon's rising, the flags flying and the drums.
Peace at last for the small people, a new age, though dull
not such as I would have chosen, such as must come.

Yet the past remains, and the rock bound earth
as I bear witness, the long pull
backwards and downwards through the buried cultures.
How can I fail them, having made in me
the slow-formed structure of retina and tongue?

Up here, the festival of sun and deliverance
the children march in white, the dead are buried
among the hats and white ball dresses, the hot nest
of love affairs, the stale
reek of family feuds, their whole antique armoury.

As yet, you have no tongue, no eye
to articulate the new, and grasp it.
I am your eye and tongue.

And old habits reform under new words
old styles creep back to their assured places
past inattentive sentries. In the cringe
of an insolent servant, a whole unspoken paradigm.
The sun beats in vain upon the rock bound earth.

I would pull you all down under the earth.

[1975, MS-2674/110]

'IN WASHING DISHES, SHE SOUGHT HER USUAL END'

In washing dishes, she sought her usual end:
it's never-ending, would say: yet no dish-racks for her:
each plate firmly, brightly, towelled and stacked
with its set of six in the crockery cupboard, the forks,
polished as for some bronze-age burial, side by side.
Her kitchen, so, at day's end was an exhibition:
the taps all polished and the sink-top dry
no toys littered the floor, food scraps packeted
in small neat shrouds of newsprint filled the dustbin.
A final glance around the kitchen, then the light switch—
the morrow chaos again of broken shells, dissolving crusts.

Was it joy then at fulfilment stabbed her one day's end
between sink and crockery cupboard, mouth wide with disbelief
at the loud tap filling the sink brimful and overflowing?

[1975, MS-2674/110]

TERRITORIAL DISPUTE

Battered by rains through July, August, September
it is my coal and woodyard
choked with dead leaves, dust and pine-chips.

Slowly filling with sun from October onward
it becomes your Italian garden.
On the blue table there are books and sewing.

Some days, though, I'll come and turn a page
or two, in your Italian garden
and every day you thump the washing in my woodyard.

Colin took this picture of us in my woodyard
not looking at the camera, nor at your Italian garden
but at each other. We are standing outside the washhouse.

[1975, MS-2674/110]

NOW WE ARE

When you were seven you made a parachute
for your favourite stuffed dog. I forget its name
but remember that so English park: the gothic residence
awkwardly converted to a government office
with filing cabinets in the breakfast room, the lake

choked with weeds, the kitchen garden
a pony club: small pink girls squealing in the churned mud.
There were trees there, and some quite decent grass.
                       It was a kind of fun
for a Saturday in November, and the TV set not working
though the parachute hardly opened in the damp air.
One more try, and then we have to go—
but the tree was not the kind that you can climb.
It hung there, I suppose, a whole English winter
while time worked its ragged change with us.
Well, it was a long time ago. You were seven.
I am the one, thank god, who has to remember.

[1975, MS-2674/110]

HOME THOUGHTS FROM ABROAD

I tell you, there is a great bog in this country.
You will not find it on any map:
it isn't that kind of bog.
You will not see it as you look over the plains
but have you noticed how the mountain air will swallow up
    any shout?

Oh, on the street corner
do not shake any hand
be careful how you pass the time of day.
The man whose hand you take is already drowning:
see the grin close over his face. He is a bog person.

Do not offer yourself:
to offer yourself is to hurl a stone
at the green face of a bog.

It makes a fine parabola but
the bog swallows it down without even a belch.
What point is there in making fine parabolas?

Imitate rather the wisdom of a tree:
explore with your roots what firm ground there is
quietly entrap with your leaves what sunlight there is.
In time you may become a piece of coal.

[MS-2674/110]

PIONEERS

My love
today I saw an old steamer
laid up and rusty against the wharf
it was
unmistakable—the two long thin funnels
of our steamer: do you remember the days
we sailed interminably over a bright sea
land always below the horizon, ourselves hand in hand
by the rail? I think you wore a long dress
but I have forgotten. It was another century!
There were no passengers, but us
and we never came to any island
but always onward. The sea was so bright.

Things cannot last: Time has moved
so many of his pieces against us. Sometimes
I feel inside my chest something
that must surely burst. However
I am happy to tell you this: our ship's still sailing
ploughing its way through an ocean
whose name I have forgotten. You are there

wearing a long dress.
We will not come to any land.

[January 1976, MS-3619/042]

'I AM A SMALL BOY'

I am a small boy
visiting London
for the first time.
I hold my mother's hand.

My small son waits with his mother
on the other side of the globe.
If you do not hurry
I shall be grown up.

I shall be gone.

[29 January 1976, MS-3619/042]

'A BEAUTIFUL DARK HAIRED GIRL RUNS'

A beautiful dark haired girl runs
distraught through the station
concourse, crying, her face
fragmented by grief.

An African woman sees me put
my ticket in the wrong way: I
catch her eye, and her face becomes
suddenly beautiful and warm as
she laughs at me.

[MS-3619/042]

A DULL MAN, ESSENTIALLY

She lies sleeping now
in the other room
her lips parted and her hands turned down.
Her breathing regular.

All my life I have been a dull man
blowing a tiny balloon
into a huge excitement of colour.

All my life I have been a dull man.
One's nature's what one escapes into eventually:
the nearest bolthole
but not necessarily the safest.

She lies in the other room.
There were two places, twelve years apart:
the day we drove up the Pacific Highway
and stopped to swim at a sunlit bay
bare feet tender on hot sand, on knife-edged rock
and then on the car's pedals.
There was sand in the car, sand on our limbs:
we did not stop to change, or to consider.
The trees and streams flashed by and were eternal.

Now this: far below in the night
the hills outlined by necklaces of light
the liner floodlit at her berth
and a ferry moving slowly seaward
between the dark hills.
Two places, both strange, and twelve years apart
and a woman lying asleep in the other room.

[March 1977, MS-3619/042]

YOUR STORY

a gesture engraved upon air
an idea for organising cells
an ache in the nerves
a pause in the hall of memory
before a papered-over door

darkness spreading upon paper
the poplar, heard trembling
throughout the still night
a stream clasped in the arms
a black tunnel under water
a snowflake in the fire
the moon beyond frosted glass

knowledge, carried carefully
as a small blue egg in the hand

[c. March 1983, MS-3619/009]

JAZZ RECORD REQUESTS

How archaic now the clipped syllables
of the bebop singer! Why must we always dig
up that old stuff? I see us as children:
me with freckles and downy face, prowling
through thickets of uncertainty
you in a fenced garden, thin arms and legs
in a print dress, working among
tropical flowers and insects, more remote
in childhood than in death. It seems
no amount of later knowledge, equating of dates
and photographs could bring us together
or plausibly join our hands.

Other fashions came later, eponyms of ages
briefer than Saturn's, when men lived well.
In one such we met, its nomenclature
lost to men now, a negative epoch, memorable
for a war that didn't happen and our October passion
—remote now too, but making its unappeasable claims.
Would we have recognised then
our latter selves in pictures blurred
by the habits we caught from each other and distorted
so sixties, and seventies, led us to this late
most winning of fashions: what would you have made
of my strong solitude, I of your breathless surrender
to death's most accomplished techniques?

So many fashions coming and going: the world
speeds up to relegate us both
to an archaic time. The cost is small
(you were still young) for pain to acquire
so ancient a patina: there we are
in our elegiac poses, statues in a formal garden
of grief, having our rightness in the world
and there, peering up at them hand in hand
the children who never met, nor wished to understand.

[MS-3619/009]

A SUMMER NIGHT

This music takes me back five years
a summer night, a party.
I knew what clothes you were wearing
the long skirt, the sandals.

I remember you putting them on
but cannot remember you taking them off
just as I cannot remember our making love
though certain that we did
taking that, like much else, for granted
and I see now what the music was saying
and why it seemed to be pointing
beyond the laughter, the open windows, the summer night
to a precise destination of solitude.

[25 March 1983, MS-3619/012]

'WHITLEY ROCKS'

Your picture is glowing tonight—
colours I never noticed when you were alive.

How we would argue about the time of day!
It is evening, I would say, deepening into night:
a calm night.

No, you would say, it is morning!
Sun-blink on a wild sea, a promise
of wilder weather to come.
Unquestionably, morning.

Now you have turned into my night,
alone on the shore I face your wild morning.

[25 March 1983, MS-3619/012]

FRIENDS AT THE FUNERAL

I pause before each of you, folding your hands together
between my two, and hold them there.

For us, that's an intimate gesture: her death
makes both of us into lovers.

My words, though, are formal, but at the sixth or seventh
are suddenly stopped: now I have shown you my tears.

You too respond: hands meet, then eyes: in this cold plot
suddenly we melt together.

How I hate you all for missing the point:
her absence has made you strangers.

You gather like crows:
I see now why you have come: in black irregular clusters

you spill out your long sentence upon the snow.

[14 April 1983, MS-3619/012]

WINTER STRAWBERRIES

There were winter strawberries in the market today:
first of a new season. I saw them and pushed between
the old couples leaning together like trees
to the fruit girls sorting among mounds of yellow and green

and bought them as if for you, remembering how you poised
one on the end of a spoon before putting it to your lips
reciting 'Goldilocks' in dry self-mockery
but in a silence I could not enter without a prayer perhaps

that next year's strawberries might bring time round again
with its new life gift-wrapped in a familiar past.
Friends tell me now how the dead survive in memory:
but what memory could surprise us with such novelty of taste?

[14 April 1983, MS-3619/012]

THIRD PARTY

Impulsive, as ever
grabbing at what seemed always
about to slip away
neither of us read the small print—

'one will desert the other
at a time unspecified
and not necessarily convenient to either.'

Should we have thought twice?
We always knew what the small print said.

[16 April 1983, MS-3619/009]

SAYING AND MEANING

You told me of this poet once:
                              'I like him,' you said.
You did not say 'I wish you'd read him too'
though that was what you meant. I took your book
and tried it for a while, but pushed it aside
wondering at you, but more at myself
and at time that puts things out of joint.

That was some years ago. I've taken the book again
looking for ways to say what can't be said
and find a guide who seems to understand
better than we could have guessed, when paths diverge
and finally diverge and one continues on
what he, or she, might need.
                              Was it that you meant?
Mastery or a skill with abstract things? I'd say the latter
but I'll never know. In any case
it took that much to make me pay attention
to whichever priceless gift you offered me.

I'd like, now, simply to look up at you
sitting across this room and hand back your book
altered in the way you wanted it.

[21 April 1983, MS-3619/009]

HOMOEOTELEUTON

The pathway on this headland
Strangely retraces
The pathway on that headland
A hemisphere away:
Two springs: there
The sparkle
Of granite among heather
And the green Atlantic

Here hot sandstone and the dazzle
To one pair of feet.

We were
Old and sober enough
To promise without rhetoric
Unending renewal of love—
Redeemed for us here
In the thunder of surf
And one pair of ears.

[Manly, 11 August 1983, MS-3619/012]

VI ∾ Courting Death (1984)

'WHY, WHEN I SPEAK, DO YOU NEVER ANSWER?'

There is this dialogue
which appears to go on between us:
it will not bear examination
and never says anything new.

I am cobbling it together
out of old photographs and bits of clothing
a dog-eared notebook, a learned habit
a gesture left hanging in the empty air.

It is a primitive device
and has its dignity: something a stranger
would treat with respect
coming across it in a desolate place.

ANOMALOUS BEHAVIOUR

Grief is stronger than fear:
that much the cock pheasant said
as we shifted his fluttering mate
to the roadside and waited for her to die.

His round eye watched us
as he circled about her, courting death
we would have said, if that eye
had not been so opaque

unable to tell us whether grief
is more than anomalous behaviour, nor
what changes lay beyond the dry-
stone wall, for mindless birds, for ourselves.

POINT OF NO RETURN

We took flight at last
as we said we would
flying westward, disencumbered

above the thunderclouds
and the turmoil of the elements
in the taut fuselage of our skins

we reached the furthest point
flying six miles high
higher than any condor.

It was what we had come to see
but then you fell to earth:
I watched you, turning over and over

the faintest white speck in the blue
then the many white specks of which blue is made
in the end, only the blue.

BY FOREIGN HANDS

You lay in a blue chapel
under blue sheets drawn to the chin
your hands not showing.
Someone else had done your hair
ignorantly parting
it on the wrong side.

Someone else had done your hair
and arranged your hands and tucked you up in bed

and done your hair and done your skin and done your eyes

your long, asymmetrical feet

expertly composing what was to be composed
expertly parting what was to be parted

[15 April 1983]

FIVE O'CLOCK

1

This is the hour
when you do not come home each night
when your key does not turn in the lock
and your bag does not thump down in the hall.
This is the hour when nothing happens.
This is an evil hour.

2

The telephone rings:
voices ask how am I.
Oh I am very well thank you.
No, I am not at all well:
there is this silence in my head.

3

This is an evil hour.
This is an evil place
only to be described by negatives.
One day I shall praise its love and justice.

4

This is what you have left me:
our son's two eyes.
I look into those orbs of black fire
wondering where you are in the world beyond them.

CREATURES OF THE FIRE

You cannot look upon me here
but I can invent ways
of resuming you
hot, radiant, and particular:
take me, you shout, I am melting!
The fire spouts from all your caverns
your mouth is shaped for singing.

GHOSTS

> *And Achilles leapt up and said,* o popoi,
> *I see that even in the House of the Dead
> there is a soul and a ghost, but there
> is no mind in it at all.*

1

You follow behind
always at the same distance
perhaps twenty yards.

When I stop to look at the hills
you stop too
and wait till I go on.

Around your thin shape
rags flutter in the wind;
in my head I can see your face:

it is thin, dun-coloured
the eyes too large
and the mouth agape with grief.

When I turn, you sidle away
a shadow into the light
but your wail persists in my head

like wind in black heather
devouring me with your sadness.
I would prefer to be afraid.

2

Only your questions remain:
they drift into my head
and dance like leaves:

'What is the world made of these days?'

'Of classes and numbers, as always.
Of colours and sounds, as always.
Of the class of colours you cannot see
and sounds you cannot number.

It is, as always,
the sum of all things minus one.
It is not a world you would recognise.
It exists in my head.
It was never any different.'

3

Ghosts exist.
Ghosts are not illusions.
We make ghosts with our minds.

They are out there.
They live in Hades.
They drink blood
and squeak like bats.

They are less real than gods
who do not need blood
but more real than humans
who cannot live without it.

Ghosts do not harm us
they only ask for a pity
we are unable to give.

Ghosts exist.
Ghosts make us with their minds.

[16 April 1983]

4

You are there
dressing in a corner
drawing on a stocking
your foot on that chair

here too in the vacant
space beside me in my bed:
I put out my hand
to feel the pulse in your head

under my hand it trembles and leaps
a small furred animal.
The sheets are cool:
the bed, the corner empty.

There you are again:
a dress has taken your shape.
Rest: soon I shall be gone
the room, the house empty.

5

Astringent Greek ghost
bitter on tongue
palpable: rock
dry: sun

dried leather in sun
thirsty: ash
brine crust, olive root
sea once washed

pungent smoke: fig wood
sharp blue thistle
blood smear on hand
needle threading the nostril

fire blackened and twisted
wire root of heather
snaring the swift runner
fading with breath.

6

Why do you drive me out
of my mind with your complaints?
I was not there to catch you when you fell
nor to hear your last words.
I did not take that care of you
which you once, formally, requested.
I have not buried you properly:
your soul stands shivering on a wet bank.
I have not yet washed your underwear:
I have not straightened this drawer
nor written to that friend.
I have not read the book you gave me
nor tried to understand your work.
I have forgotten the thing you once told me.

Oh rest, perturbed spirit:
all shall be set straight at last
with precision and magnificence.

7

You take over my decisions, my movements:
making the breakfast
buttering the toast
or putting our son to bed
I feel you driving my forearms
striving to see through my eyes:
I knock jugs over, fail to see what's there.

I would not mind being you
and I would gladly have changed places
but it will not work:
this way, I am haunted.

It is not that you are angry:
I could endure your anger.
Not your dumb distress at not being here
to do what needs to be done
over and over and over.

8

I look up, you are coming down the stairs
I know your sandal's creak
and the swirl of your skirt around your knees.
I know everything about you.
Now you are half way down
soon our hands will meet.

Poor ghost, when will I let you sleep?

9

Last night you slept in this bed
say twelve hours ago.
But your time stopped
say a hundred years ago.
Stale Victorian ghost
you thud and boom in the chimney.
Stale ghost, you awaken me
to a science fiction century
where metal clothes are worn
and grammar has lost the moods of regret.
Lightning made its photogravure here:
its blue light robbed colour from your lips
as its heat froze your heart's movement.
Your time stopped this morning.
The wind thuds in the chimney.
The world is made of such statements.

TONIGHT

rain comes again, and wind to sweep the rain
along the pavement where we carried you:
as if they bent to this small cleansing task

till there's nothing but black granite in the rain.
I close the curtain and am comforted
as if there had been something there to wash

though there was nothing. It takes years of rain
to wash away an image from the mind:
slowly it forms again, as in the tales

which men invent of shadows no-one casts
or stains that will not go away.
I'm comforted, all the same. There's something else

that's stated by the wind and rain out there
that have come before and will come and come again.

CUPBOARD LOVE

Gradually we deplete the larder
of all the stock you left us.
Jars are emptied and recycled one by one,
tawdry packets replace them, sometimes we try
a new brand, but slowly
the spaces between them grow. Even the arrangement
changes: ideas are always the last things to go.

I like the economy of this tidy larder.
I like things to be used and used up and done with.

What are we to do with your vast untidy love
that fills every room and corner of this house like the sea
in a sinking ship and can never be exhausted?

TRAVEL DIARY

You will not look
at those Turners again
nor a hundred paintings of Italy
and these pages blankly waiting
for your notes upon them:
so little equipment
so carefully assembled
the five senses
educated in a plain school
and so much of the soul
going into pencils and pens
which the soul then deserts
untouched by their disarray.
Your tears were always reserved
for the disappointment of others
never for your own.

[5 May 1983]

A POSTCARD OF CORNWALL

The harbour wall, sunlight on the water
the blue boats, and the bookshop of a lost language—
I can feel you taking it all.

Look, already the colours fade in the mind:
only the name stays to signify a place
where two made love in the deep grass of June.

Were they really ourselves? Gently, persistently
I feel you working at it, working it all away
under the bright surface that divides our elements.

Soon, if you go on like this
I shall have nothing left. Take it, then:
or anything that helps.

Your needs are unimaginable. The sun-
filled estuary, widening to the sea—
take it all. Take me.

[5 March 1983]

ON THE EQUATOR

The memory of your voice is fading
like this moon which sinks upon the edge of the world:
soon it will be entirely gone.

This is a priceless moment, not given to many:
holding those poles together in the hand
whose lightning is knowledge. A hundred miles

eastward is a coast of fevers
choked by low trees and inhabited by snakes:
the sailors sniff it on the warm night breeze

and keep their offing.
                        The moon is gone.
Indifferent to minor pains and insights
our darkened liner dips gently southward.

VII ∾ The Classic Cast of Grief

che t'amo tanto
ch'usci per te della volgare schiera?

—Dante, *Inferno*, II:104–05

PURAKANUI BIRDCALL

for Alyth

Warbler
over
water
green
translucent
over
sand
golden
warbler
over
gorse
blazing
golden-
      green
pine
      green-
black
pine   over
water
green
translucent
over
sand
golden
green

over
water
warbler
green.

Over.

[MS-2674/187]

THE DIVIDE

We took the inland route, against
all advice, and it was murder:
the gradients, the dangerous bends, a child
crying for a book left behind, my shirt

sticking to my back. The road climbed
the heat climbed. When we reached the divide
there was nothing to see but flat baked pastures
and three eagles hanging from a rusty fence.

Next morning at the hotel we woke to rain
and a lump of hill covered with sodden bush.
Looking down from the verandah at the drops
glazing our new car, I felt time's shift

and it was down hill all the way: the rain
the roadblocks, police in their streaming capes.
The lights were on when we came to the city
driving blind into the map of our future.

[MS-2674/187, 22 May 1983 variant MS-2674/185]

TRUTH

If you should enter now
heralded by this cold draught
I would not be afraid

but curious rather
would wait respectfully
for you to speak

hugging the discreet joy
of the true scientist
who sees his hypothesis upset.

The draught is just a draught.
I did not think that you would enter
or choose cold to be your herald.

[MS-2674/184, MS-2674/185, MS-2674/187]

INTERVIEWS OF EYES

At the last moment, your eyes
grow too preoccupied
to spare a glance for the world:

turning inward instead
upon a private theatre
where your whole being is entertained

reminding me of other such moments
as when we lose all need
for the interviews of eyes

in the proximity of atoms flying
beyond each other for ever
at the speed of light.

[MS-2674/184, MS-2674/187]

LIFELIKE

'That was how it was, it was just like that:
I came home by a late train from Oxford
From talking to a scholar who had lost her mind
Unable to release a lifetime's notes locked there.

We made love and watched *Krapp's Last Tape* on TV.
I am not making this up.
Next morning was like spring though a week to Christmas:
you danced in the air and picked up a summer blouse.

When I came downstairs your eyes had stopped trying to find us.
Later I got back a plastic bag full of clothing.
I am not making this up
And shall not need to, ever again.'

[MS-2674/184, MS-2674/187]

DEATH PORNO

I am watching you write a poem
you are watching me write a poem
the poem is called *Death porno*
and is about life under the Nazis.

How would I have behaved under the Nazis?
Who knows how any of us would have behaved?
I watch you twist and turn under me:
anyone would think you were trying to escape.

I am wearing my leather, my officer's talc:
that smell of shit could perfume a whole decade.
You are wearing stockings of field grey
your Lili Marlene hat.

Everywhere there are blossoms
the streets are full of bicycles and yellow tramcars
glass doors swing in and out
people are smiling everywhere.

Next, I shall be underneath
in my Luftwaffe camisole.
You will bestride me
in your rakish lieutenant's cap.

How else could we behave?
Anyone would think that we liked it
this long collaboration
this slow methodical tunnelling.

[MS-2674/187, variant MS-2674/185]

'AND IN THAT WAY'

1

and in that way
the wine
was spilt
    cas-
cading over the shelf
the cupboards
wall
falling
to the floor: no
calling it back
conjuring it up
into the bottle
again
    it spreads
and spreads.

2

something's always
on the watch for
a lack of care
because accid-
accidents
will happen
        the tongue
stuttering
        the hand
mistiming
        the note

mis-sung
        the breath
missing
not there when needed
and something opens
unstitched in time
and the god let out
years watching
for such a chance
no fighting
divine patience
the cunning of gods.

3

But law again
is something different
not god not human:
the apple falling
a mathematician's
or an emperor's,
singing praise
to the earth that bore it
and calls it back
as love calls.
Law is different
and time is what
we mostly know
as irreversible
time that flows
like wine like blood
unlike love

calls nothing back
but pushes onward
like blood, and blood
like wine gets spilt
falls
and falls
and singing falls.

   4

Only
the song's line
rising and falling
and rising again
inviting us to a journey
embarking us for
the island of love
where even the silliest
are transfigured
only the song
drawing us onward
to a natural end
back to the note
where it all began
only song
conjuring up
the blood from the floor
defeating time

in time.

[September–November 1984, MS-2674/187]

TALENT

Not one of these poems is good:
not one will reach that distinction
to which they set out like younger sons.
Finding you once was their only talent
now that death is your disguise
you will not come back for them
in that form
nor in this.
But death too has to be waited for
or journeyed to in discomfort
as if it were a reward
though there's nothing to see when you get there.

Everyone's travelling, these days.

[MS-2674/187]

DUAL NUMBER

The two of you
in your doorway:
goodnight
goodnight

the house behind
a shared life
of secret rooms.

Fortunate, I thought
all the way home

remembering the talk
in your study with its chairs
like two thrones
and beyond it the black

silence of water.

[MS-2674/186]

BRICOLAGE

   1 Green Bottle

And then again, this endless need I have
to talk to you, as if ears could be marble,
immortal, as if we didn't know them gristle
where all the words of Mercury are dulled.
As if I didn't know. Tonight, as I unseal
another bottle, I notice on the foil
a name from Scotland where we watched—like green
tourists who expect to live for ever!—
green ranks of bottles marching to their fate.
Endless. Things keep arriving from that past:
Today, the abstract of your thesis, pared
to a slim eloquence, your mind's true marble.
The foil clings to my fingers, all night I share
my pillow with its acrid smell, word verdigris.

   2 Cardboard Box

I unpack such things from memory, and wonder
why I do it—wouldn't it be simpler
to leave them lying in their stiff brown box?

Old diaries, photographs, a walk by a summer lake
a walk by a winter lake, this time alone
wind cutting up the water and brown leaves.
Why kneel here over this box of small obsession
taking out the instruments, laying them back,
contracted to a ritual? Why not let
the mind expand, by lakeshores, under skies
something other than that white reversal
that emptying out of all they ever contained?
Why isn't it enough to be alone?
         To grieve
must be like religion, like the love of God.

3 Cut Glass I

Your mind is filled with dusty *bric a brac*,
but set it all down, *bricoleur*:
         this blue
glass inkwell, set on the windowledge to catch
the moon's glint on its pointed stopper like
the minaret in the book of fairy tales—
the princess and the prince who sang to her.
She left it as a gift one hard September
setting foot forever on her ship to Europe
but turning to a bird was there again
next dawn, in crumpled feathers, at his door
claiming it, and him, forever, never,
a fairy tale!
    … and has withdrawn
farther than Europe, farther than the moon
leaving the glass, a cool light drifting through …

4 Cut Glass II

Your blue glass catches the moon—so far, so far
from the moon to it, so near from it to you
and still these spaces are commensurable
telling you why you're here: it is to learn
how the world will look once you have left.
It takes only the shortest time to learn
what it must be to look like that for ever.
It must be learned again with each new day:
until it is learned, the world is incomplete,
a moonlight clinging to the shape of things
that turn their backs on us for ever.
                              O high white bird
catching the sun, beyond the spire of night!

5 Wrack

Not able to live with the here and now, my mind's
like the sea that day, clawing at the barnacled rock
for handhold, losing it, making a grab again
for what seems real: your bare foot, brown on that rock
then thinned to a wavering image no-one shares.
Other things from that day: the sea's blue tilt
the sandstone crumbling against our skin
the curve of your upper lip, burnt brown that season—
you were like driftwood sea and sun had polished
in their godlike work of making things immortal.

These are your true ghosts. How much of the commonplace
does it take to live in a world where everything disappears?
Bits of us fly into space, and we gape stupid
like the soldier holding the boot that holds his foot.

6 Cranach: Adam and Eve

You deal kindly with me today: sliding
from bed first thing, I found your ready words
take precedence in my throat before I knew,
ring crisply in the cavern of my head.
So all day on, with tasks we would have shared
on any Saturday: washing and pegging out,
the half hour stolen with coffee and our books—
poised sideways on our chairs and waiting nervous
for God's awful minute to lay its claim.
This was to be one again, the fruit of summers'
coupling, and then uncoupling, by those beaches:
not ripened until now. The peaceful Saturdays of winter!
The smoke of bonfires rising straight
into the still grey sky! Tomorrow can pour its rain
into the split fruit rotting under trees.

7 Dolce vita

Coming down upon Stockton from the North York moors
gliding from drystone to an industrial landscape
the sky a cold green, clouds swimming in the Tees
among the stacks of ICI: 'it's not the places
but the company that matters': you beside me,
our taking that for granted. The changing light
broke in green waves upon your peaceful face:
there was no change that could not enrich us—
it was for us those wheels were spinning!

Today on another moor I see walls tumbled
for want of poor men's art, and whistling birds
take off for nowhere. From an empty sky
a sentence comes spinning back: 'Last night, for me,
the Muse took off her pantyhose and I knew I'd made it.'

[MS-2674/186, variant MS-2674/185, MS-2674/187, MS-4150/001, section 6 as]

THINGS NO LONGER SIMPLE

Things that are no longer simple
that I knew once like the back of my hand
or better yours, that I had more reason to study:
its fine bones, its veins close under the skin—

which is now nowhere and how can I ever
teach myself to believe that?
So I study things all the more, and hope
that all will grow familiar again as hands—o but what
hands do you wear now, what language can you speak
that is yours only, but everyone understands?

[MS-2674/186, variant MS-2674/187, MS-2674/185]

SECOND CHANCE

You, once in your life, became able
to see and to describe
the shape and colour of hope.

Declaring it to be oval
the colour blue:
a bed of flowers, a stone.

That was just before you lost it
or so you thought: later
it was there again

in roughly the same colour and shape
as what you'd changed it for:
enduring, and much less.

[MS-2674/187]

LINES ON A PHOTOGRAPH

1

I have discovered this marvellous poet—
Italian: you would have liked him
for that and a world of reasons
into which it is strange you never entered.
Stranger, that we shall never ask your opinion.

2

One portrait hangs on the black wall of my mind:
that one in which the two of us
awkwardly support a heavy gilt frame
and gaze through it at the photographer.
Our faces are unsuitably pinched
for such an amusing occasion:
but the North London garden was damp
the photographer more than a friend
with his own difficult way of seeing us.

3

I understand what is wrong:
we keep thinking of you as that magical guest
whose prolonged absence is inexplicable
but who will, undoubtedly, turn up
with a new amusing adventure to tell us.
Meanwhile, the party is a frost
the guests locked in agonies of silent laughter
and nothing will ever happen again.

4

In fact you were always that quite different
person whom death permits us to glimpse
by putting a frame around her unfinished life—
we see her now not looking at us at all
but heading out on some separate occasion
to that horizon sheeted in grey
leaving us to our discomfort, awkwardly trying
to account for our presence in the frame.

[MS-2674/187]

from 3½ POEMS ABOUT THE WEATHER FOR R.

1 I'm glad you rang

All the starlings on all the telephone wires in the world
turn into ridiculous bells
and fly off squawking. You no longer hear
the norwester thrumming from headland to headland.

A brimming tide
has drowned the psalmsong from the cave: for once
the voices of the dead aren't tolling
through the sea's long fall.

A seriousness is there: it hangs in the north west
where clouds darken like slow bruises.
Meanwhile this feathery
light enfolds us in the softest of arms.

   2 I like you a lot

Like a stroke of lightning
you set all the telephone bells ringing
when you say it carefully, but just now

I'm re-reading this biography
which says that there were others as well
besides that one, that famous affair

everyone remembers: these details strike
on a second reading.
                     Look before you leap
is what your words are saying, but I've already

leapt: along the horizon lightning blinks
like a huge eye and the bells are ringing madly.
No fool like a young fool.

3½ Can we meet again sometime?

The weather advances
the weather goes back.
It's always there. The sun
pushes a finger through the cloud:
the cloud
goes into another cloud. You
are always there, always becoming.
You, and you and you.

[MS-2674/187]

HERE IS MY SONG FOR DEATH: LYDIAN CHANT

Here is my song for death:
I think he will come soon.
Here is my song for death, and for my friends:
I think death will come soon
Oh I hope that he will come soon.
Here is my song for my friends
to tell them that I saw death coming—
I walked through the gate to greet him
like a courteous host, like an old friend.
Here is my song for my friends
Oh here is my song for my friends.
And we talked in the road, like friends
standing in the sun, we talked in the road.
I saw death coming, and went to greet him
not being a stone, a mindless thing.
Here is my song for death

Here is my song for my friends
I saw him coming, and greeted him
Like a courteous host, not like a stone
Not like a stone, like one who knows death
Who has welcomed death, who has given death food and drink
And entertained him, and watched him go.
Here is my song for my friends
Here is my song for death
My song for death who comes soon
For death who comes late and soon.

[MS-2674/185]

THE FIRST OF MARCH

The wind gets up tonight
splashing the red of leaves
on pane and patio
waking the ordered garden
the serene madness of summer
to news of change and flood.
You are cut out of these changes
now, and are not gone
your absence the nerve that jars
in each dislocation.
There is so much of this world
you would have understood
that I must let flow past
with leaves on the stream
I cannot put together
in the book of prophecies.

I cannot complete your work
nor rest until I do
being that mind which failed you
and carries your discontent
until it can die too.

[MS-2674/184, variant MS-2674/185, MS-2674/187]

'BUT'

But
somewhere
up there above
that hill, beyond
all those trees, behind
that towering cloud you are forever
putting things into an oven, talking
to a child, kneeling in a pink dress
your hair hanging down
in the sun of a particular afternoon

And
slowly
I am overtaking
the hill, the trees
the cloud, getting nearer
all the time, soon
I shall have passed the corner where time
can hold things apart any longer, soon
everything will fly together irresistibly

[MS-2674/184, variant MS-2674/185, MS-2674/187]

CONVERSATION

There is something
that keeps one going—love,
love of god, love of the good
patriotism, or just
our good manners:
good morning, good evening, yes
very well, thank you

and under that, something else
resembling a river
dark, resistless as fear
stubborn as a bad habit

and this survives
all the important deaths: of love
of the beloved, of country
of any belief
in goodness or in god
even perhaps
the importance of manners

Aristotle said
that anyone outside society
and not needing it was either
a beast or a god:
some kinds of loss
can reduce or exalt: think
of Timon, think
of Oedipus.

But under
all this the river:
its raw edge

rasping away
at the raw things of love
at anything
we choose as human
at dignity, at affection
converting
everything back to mud
trumpeting it to sea

[MS-2674/185]

'THE EVENINGS ARE HOT'

The evenings are hot. Hotter, I think, as the summer advances.
Most evenings I sit and work by an open window.
Mostly I'm correcting misprints, trivial errors, orthography,
matters like that—I don't mean the systematic mistakes
introduced into an Author's Work by the B-translation
that strange source of anomaly, so wild, yet so contented
such an odd reflection of what one knows to be right
that one could almost review the Author himself—
but I'll be leaving all that for the Preface and next spring.
So hot, these evenings. Yet night comes earlier now
only 3 weeks to the equinox. There's been no rain.
The corrections are tedious, but a necessary task.
I'm getting on, though slowly. By the beginning of winter
I should be up to *our* great scene, where the Author
writes us in, his major characters. You remember the dialogue
how it goes on, yet never repeated, nothing
in six great speeches, standing upon one another
like the strata of a pyramid, always that sense
of working to a definitive statement—

I won't tell you, also my researches have enabled me
not only to solve the famous crux: I have a theory
about what went wrong, and where. It should
remove *all* that was puzzling about the central scene,
and I mean all. It's uncanny, as if
I was rewriting, the way the Author himself—
I can't tell you how exciting. Yes. I should sing …
I'll be getting there about the middle of winter.

[MS-2674/187]

THE BLANKNESS OF SNOW

The snow looming at night through frosted glass
in the bathroom is white without shape

let the water run over long hands and stare
in the mirror thinking of nothing

white the water runs and the steam grows thick
and the neon light glares back from the yellow tiles

and absurd fish swimming on blue flannels
and children's toys and an empty sponge bag.

Bathrooms are for solitude: for waking up in
for crying and sometimes for dying in

and other acts we prefer to do in private
but slight things, all of them, beside the whiteness

that stares through the window and has no shape
and is as close as we can get to the thought of nothing.

[MS-2674/187]

HAUNTED HOUSE

Passing the grey stone farmhouse
on our walk to Shaftoe Crags you commented:
you never wanted to own a house before.

Later that month you closed your eyes.
And walking up to the house you opened door after door
taking formal possession of each room in turn.

Now the house is never still, hearing in every room
the swish of your skirt and your quick step receding
night after night its windows blaze over the valley.

[MS-2674/187]

THE HOUSE OF CHILDHOOD

I watched you walk along that mile of beach
to the house at the end of the beach

the home I'd pointed out, the house of childhood.
How well I remembered the garden, its grey stone wall
the stone rest in the garden, overlooking the sea.

And so you set off bravely, to walk that mile
staggering now and then in the sand that ran to you until
the sun blazed overhead, to the right the sea shimmered
I watched you walking that mile, your figure grew smaller and
    smaller.

Out of the sea's shimmer came the faint crying
of voices subdued by the sea and the view.
I remembered the stone rest, the thyme scent of the garden
and beyond the stone wall, the sea splashing in the evening.

I pointed all this out to you, this house of my childhood
and watched you set off towards it, staggering slightly
not looking back, growing smaller and smaller
until you passed into the sand, into the stone wall

and under the garden, the earth of the garden, under the sea.

[MS-2674/186]

WAIKANAE, WITH VANESSA AND TOBY

The sea
dumps its sand briskly
then goes back for more.
Fifteen seconds later
it dumps its sand again.
It's a small busy animal
and knows what it's about.

Out there, Kapiti
trails cloud vaguely from its peak.
It could be an Italian steamer.
It could be Capri. It could be Ithaca.
The sea however
has it all quite clear.
It allows islands to be anything.

[January 1985, MS-2674/185, MS-4150/008]

VIII ∾ The Entrance to Purgatory (1986)

Everything longs to return to its own beginning.

—Dante

Part One

FLYING BACK

   1 Rome 1965

'The pines aren't Respighi's
but could be: the wind's getting up
in light scuffles among the cones
on the fountain
water tautens like skin.
Clouds have no identity
photographs little and the wind
may serve as proof for the existence of nothing.
Nothing's unique nor of a certain age
if not the music, and that only
so long as you choose to listen: it was
the transistors switching off one by one
made Saint Augustine afraid to die.'

These were the words your picture spoke
smiling from a terrace above
the Eternal City, your legs
made thin by love, your hair showing
which way the wind was already blowing.

   2 Pieces of Occasion

To this uncentred self the world of strangers
can seem at times merely your room untidied,
books and underwear trailing you over the floor
to where you went out and did not return—

so unlike you. I'm picking up the pieces
still. Reports arrive in letters
telling me things I can't hear in your voice
though I say them to myself over and over—

Tonight, your words saved from the memorial service
'I do not dare to hope': a fragment
to stop the heart, yet one never unearthed
in all the long hunt through a year of cantos

and beds of strangers. But not to know for sure!
Such phrases may be uttered lightly
like a hand patting an old sleeve. They step
down from their lettered frames, wearing fine lace

and are always someone else's. O million
faceted soul, are all our words like that,
mere pieces of occasion, subtly discredited
by a fall in interest, death's change of fashion?

   3 Flying Back

Encased in our winged time machine
we too are made privy to history through
perfected modern windows, framed
by the consolations of technology: the deltas,
twin rivers and puckered landscape of
a seminal civilisation, a millennium
modelled in plasticine. To the left
Mount Ararat; ahead, flexed like a scorpion's sting
the long tail of Cyprus where a dangerous
goddess was born, and small men burrowed for metals.
One sees this only once: the flat historical atlas
left open on the table at home growing texture
like a mould: the map becoming vision, entering

the time-bound eye
with a haze of blue, clouds, light that is never still.

Sharing our airline breakfast, like Zeus and Hera
we vary our divine concerns with glances
at the headlines of history: a block of apartments
expanding in dust, an ancient cemetery
yielding its dead to mortar fire; at icy wingtip
one of the smaller capitals of Europe
with its yellow tramcars, stainless steel art
and the skyblue uniforms
of its secret police. A new literature of protest
is made our own, entering our lives without pain: surely
we shall live for ever? Soon
(cloud over the Alps, northern Europe
wrapped in grey cotton wool) there will be nothing
further for the eye to see, we can sleep
until the landing through insistent rain
and the brown light that will not leave us now, the days
shortening towards winter. We are taking for granted
like the suitcases we carry, our right to pass
through the barriers of history and disembark uninfected
by the tiny deaths its instances forecast.

[Section 3: 27 February 1985]

DEAD LETTER

Your card came, over a year too late
with its news of houses, children grown
to amazement, the futures scattering
brilliantly, and contentments shared around
among the middle-aged.

The card was not addressed to me
but I answered it: it seemed important
to stop that ignorance, as if death too
was an achievement to be shared,
a picture of the real.

No answer comes: from the other end of the world
an appalled silence.
I fold it, and put it away
among the other silences. Perhaps
my picture showed too much:

you would have preferred
to choose your own: the hand raised in farewell
the mouth smiling, but the heel already turned
back to the house, work set out upon tables
and the door standing open.

CHOICES

Here is the painting that you chose:
I've hung it in the best
light possible, although
that corner's not quite its place.

Here are your books. The bookcase
is new but the order keeps faith still
with an old contempt for order: Joyce
goes next to Lesser on aphasia.

Your favourite cup hangs from this hook
the analogue of every plain choice.
For anything further, I'm at a loss.
I drink from it sometimes, guiltily.

Your clothes, of course. What could I do
but lay them in a new-lined drawer
smelling as they did of love and you
and I could neither wear nor burn them?

That's all, I think. Anything else can find
some new place of its own. As for ourselves, it seems
decisions won't be called for. Time's
deadbeat steadies the compass in the mind.

YOUR OLD AGE

A slight accident
a bandaged leg
and a walking stick
a theatrical prop
to amuse us all
still did not stop
your walk in the wood:
the bluebells
as you passed
drew back in comment
upon an invisible wind
then nodded forward to stillness.

So brief your old age:
a project considered
and quietly rejected.

THE FROG PRINCE

You have left your book
face down on the bedroom mat
halfway between bed and door.

This is a book from childhood.
You are asleep and will not wake
when the prince crawls into your bed.

From door to bed is a time of slow enchantment.
You will not wake when I join you.
Side by side we shall sleep forever.

VACUUM FLASK

My dreams are slow to learn:
ten months later, out of mornings
of paradisal blue they still assure me
that you are no longer dead:
you are reading a paper at a conference
you miss us all, in spite of Italy
you will be returning on the next plane.
Day brings its certainties however
in the airless gap between
the warm awareness of lives shared
and the child's cold statement of fact
'I'm crying because I won't see her again':
the boring tasks of the fairytale hero
grey paradoxes to be wrestled with and won
his ancient brides of ice.

YOUR DREAM

This is your dream: me
grizzled and shorn, a priest or prisoner
fidgeting at a table and the full moon
staring through a high window, trees
tossing outside in the silence

of a city you once knew, but
an unfamiliar part of it: girls
crouching in floodlit malls, boys with knives
an old man coughing words up on the steps
of a new century. The years running like paint.

No use begging you to wake. I can only
hope your dream won't get worse, that soon
you'll move to a deeper and colder layer
a dreamless
sleep I'll no longer know I'm sharing.

VISIT

It was too early for such a visit
and it was too late: the cheeks waxen
as flowers under glass, eyes

that had already let the world go
catching it up again in a sudden

flare of recognition—as if I
all that was in the world, could really
call back life and give it a shape

to mend the heart with—

and beyond all words now lifting arms for that
final kiss which I half refused

finding in it nothing but fever
desperation and the hardness of bone
though everything was there—

a real message, I'd say, if I believed in ghosts:
your summing up of a life shared,
its warm tangle of moods and tenses

teased out to a final simplicity:
the high persistent monotone
of memory, dream, regret.

THE WORLD OUTSIDE

This was the last
vision that you saw, these
kitchen walls, that familiar
crack running down, the homely
cups nodding like madmen
on their hooks, the blue
blaze of the gas turned up
under the kettle, an inward
fire, a light, a heat
out of nowhere.

You did not see
that famed mosaic: how it all
makes sense, fitting
down to the last
tessera: you did not say
how absurd, how wasteful
you did not wonder
about us, what
we might think: all that
arranged beforehand, concealed
like presents in luggage, or
just scattered about like clothes
waiting to be picked
up in the right order

while you shook yourself free
taking careful note how walls
are thin like paper, turning
around you while you stood still
the first time in your life: saw
the flame licking
their yellow to brown, saw
the blue-edged hole opening
the outside world at last
and a night that had swallowed
its own stars.

NIGHT GARDEN, WITH GHOST

These spring nights, you want to take off
more than clothes. Cool, cool.
The curtain sways outward, the bedroom
slides into night's privileges

its trees hung with stars, its long galleries
where the lovers sway
out of darkness into light.

A wind brushes the lips

cool hands come out of the darkness

IM WUNDERSCHÖNEN MONAT MAI

1

The portly singer clings with one hand to the piano
and when he comes to the difficult notes he rises
like a boxer swinging forward from the balls of his feet

singing very earnestly of love and of the spring
and the words are fine and the music is ah how fine
as light glints golden from his glasses and shirt buttons.

Outside the heavy church the chilled sparrows pick.
You are not here to listen, who in another autumn
in your coat and long boots went marching down to Hades.

I am here though, and hear the portly singer.
Are you envious, does your envy press against glass somewhere,
do you envy the sparrows picking on the London pavements,

do you envy me? Then why is it that I do not feel you here
filling these huge spaces with a cold like autumn
to banish for ever the words and songs of spring?

'I am here but your language has not caught up with me.
Your sentences have not learned to swing upside down
in the dark rafters of Hades where grammar breaks its back.'

2

That is no reason why I should go to bed:
if I am tired tomorrow, then I am tired.
Besides, there is only myself and the boy to look after.

Tomorrow will bring no-one to dazzle with words
no feet gliding towards me over the dew-soaked lawn:
no, not though the nightingale implore all night
till the cuckoo shatters the white mist of morning.

That is no reason why I should suddenly feel alone
though the reflection in the window is of one not old.
If I stare at it steadily, it will go away

and behind it the garden take on a green hardness
the lawn without print, and everything become clearer
as the purposeful cuckoo shouts loud toward summer.

3

Does the mouse choose to run in his wheel of wire?
Does he like the exercise, plump beady-eyed jogger?
Or does he tumble into it, on his brisk way elsewhere
finding himself trapped and paddling desperately?

I wonder about myself as about the mouse
waking each morning to a cage of silk around me
made of the skin you stepped from and the firm bones under:
my hand runs over memory as over the belly's silk.

'I didn't mean you to be caught in a silken wheel:
my intent was always to set us both free
to walk as friends in evening layers of cool and warm
not desperate like this at every flaring sunrise.'

AUTUMN THUNDER

Don't imagine that two people
can live very long in one skin:
and you've crawled into mine
like a cat out of the hailstorm
melting crystals into her black fur.

Hot evenings: one can hardly breathe.
I lean by the stove, this check apron
one you left: my mind's filled
with all the stoves you ever leaned by
your gaze melting the world to nothing

while the nights fell slowly
and one by one your lovers failed to return.
Two people can't live in one skin:
slowly, slowly they fall
these nights too hot to breathe in.

TWO NOCTURNES

   1 Dispossession: staccato

Waiting for sleep at night
my son hears
one pair of feet only
padding down the stairs:
the sound of a door opened
springs creaking in a chair
the rustling of paper
a sound that might be a cough—
not repeated—hard to tell
but certainly not laughter
nor anything that's shared;
the click of a single cup
set back on its saucer
the muffled scratch and whine
of the hi-fi set, and after
feet again on the stairs
unaccompanied by voices
to fold him from his fears.
My son, whom I call mine
meaning no-one else's
what can he think it is
that silence filling the dark
beyond the dark that's his?

2 *Possession:* legato

It is not all unpleasant, waiting for
the time to pass until it's time to go
to bed: no, really not at all
unpleasant, with the lamplight shining on
the golden Turkish rug and table piled
with brightly covered books and coffee cup
and clock that ticks so soothing from the wall
and fire that flickers and the brass that winks—

and oh it's pleasant, seeing that one's got
the room the way one wanted it: I mean
like a poet's or a scholar's, like those rooms
one's seen so often from the street: the white
sofa with no-one denting it, the script
anonymous upon the paper in the pool
of lamplight and the door behind that's just
swung to upon a life that still goes on
somewhere beyond it: scented, rich and warm
giving and taking in glad certainty
of fullness being there for ever
                                           but
felicities of view are simply signs
that something's been displaced, as feeling well
may simply mean the fever will be soon
and serious, and so it's always time
to get up and go when finally you've got
things just as right as that: yes:
                                    get up and go
and leave the room you left some time ago.

OLD FRIENDS

He stayed, and she went
taking a great deal:
their holidays together
their understanding
of the sea's blueness
its eternal blueness.

For a time all went
in the general greyness
of a few questions
which neither had asked
and had no answers
and had no answers.

It was what came back
he found surprising:
the fuss about when
about what to wear
the fuss over money
and this year or next year
year after year.

Perhaps it was merciful
but he wasn't grateful.
They helped him get by.
They were old friends:
they helped him away
on this side and that side
when he would have stayed
when he would have stayed.

ENDING THE SENTENCE

Coming down the stairs
   on ordinary mornings
     to discover death
that it exists
   and devours the past
     when it takes the future
no sudden insight
   but a gradual learning
     as the blind discover
tracing with fingers
   the shape of finality
      through repetitive days
till the heart is convinced
   no way beyond
     nothing to be said
'Today that fruit
   looked for so long
     sets longing at rest'
but first must learn
   the rote of longing
     through slow replays
(that day, those words)
   the spirit shunted
     between spool and spool
never let off
   (how can mortal stuff
     endure so long?)

but staring after
   the cool leavetaking
      the quick heel turning
in its hem of flame
   'what good can your grief
      do me, who am nothing?'
unable to exit
   from the scorpion's ring
      where love inscribed
no end to the sentence
   but mastering language
      and shift of mood.

Part Two

CRUSOE'S CANOE

for Elizabeth Smither

1

With *Everyman his owne Shipwright* in one hand
this rusted chisel in the other, I pick up
the principles as I go
              (I'm gouging a lot of trees)
We must start with detail
              (I'm wasting a lot of time)
A treenail's made from trees, that's why
it's called a treenail. Or because it holds

trees together
                (I get things half right).
First fashion your treenail: everything
is in the detail: for servants of the Lord
this holds in carnal matters: carpentry
child-begetting, the chapel's business.
From one treenail another will come
from many treenails a floatable canoe

(I am making a sensible advancement).

   2

But first you must
open your tree
up delicately
           and trees
are close things
        clinging
like one flesh, like
the firmaments
of earth and water
unwilling to be flayed
into dripping slabs.
                  Think:
your chisel's made
a new surface, displayed
its whiteness to the light.

The Lord's work, that.
Or a butcher's.

3

Do nothing for a bit: listen to the surf
and think hard about trees: how, left alone
they turn themselves into banana shapes, or how
they hold a man's curve like a hammock, ride
the big winds without going under.
Think then of canoes, how stem and prow
hold themselves together like hands in prayer:
how they'll always want to be
splaying themselves back into trees again
lying horizontal under the heavy sands

and sending up the green shoots vertical.

4

I see something of the art, it has more
of woman's witchcraft than it has of detail
a thinking yourself into things. The art
is to take trees apart in so gentle a way
that they'll hold themselves together for you
in a different shape, the living vessel
that bounces on the waves. It's not about detail—
it's more like prayer. You have to ask for the shape.
It's more like love. You have to pity the tree.
It's more like grief. You have to let things die
in their own gentle way

to sail off from the island.

WE ARE ALL IN A PAINTING

Bowing your head, you kneel
to take a book from the lowest shelf:
an attitude familiar
from paintings and religion.

Such moments of mere air
as the bending of knees, the lifting of hands
persist like meteorites
burying themselves in the sand of the heart

at the end of their flight from spaces
where the eye has no authority:
the textbook of nerves, the devious web
of arteries, cells

in their vivid primaries and other
such things as nature arranges
on shelves in her dark cupboard.
No doubt our pigments

carefully spread upon stiff canvas
will outlast them all, outlast
the tan of a knee, and beyond us
beyond the blue

of the harbour the serpentine hills are older
and have even farther to go:
yet we are all in a painting really
a chemistry of colour holds us together

and the hills are there merely to echo
the cries of us famous losers
their cypresses planted to give point
to our long option upon death

and if we look out at all, it is through
the rondure of a tear where we see ourselves suspended
in that universal solvent as the salt
of nature and of the earth.

HORACE'S GIRLFRIENDS

for Doug Little

His patron provided them, with so much else:
a house in the country, an income, books.
Some were literate: did they read his poems
which were about politics, and serious?

His tastes were polyglot: one was from Cappadocia,
one from Syria—what did they talk about,
two heads on one pillow? With no real gift for tongues
he gave them all Greek names, and stuck them into a book.

One made conditions as she took off her knickers
and was not invited again. Another
was bad for his heart, a tomboyish sea
that could toss him to nights of seasickness.

Perhaps he relished the gossip about rivals
the price of silk, the latest rock star
the sheer cattiness of it all—
such a change from manly conversations.

For they changed too, and were not easy to remember:
scholars with a theory doubt their existence.
He reproached one, though, for growing old and ugly
sounding, for once, as if he really meant it.

THEORY OF THE LEISURE CLASS, 1983

The fungus in the sky is still no bigger
than a man's finger and thumb. Meanwhile
writing tables are dragged to open windows
not to miss the blossom, so wonderful
this year. Morning's the best time
for personal correspondence, white or blue sheets
inviting to a languorous
deployment of the self. Afterwards
restored by coffee we search for brisker avocations.
We have a lot going for us, especially time:
see how it carries us forward to
dump us in the slack water of afternoon
leaving us stranded for a month
in Lotus Land. We must try to imitate the dignity
of Palladian villas, scabbed by frost and isolated
in their parks by the rings
of a receding industry. These new fashions
take some getting used to: learning to wear
our silken dressing gowns as if the stars
had laid them about our shoulders is
in itself a vocation.

A FLAT IN WC1

To chop up vegetables into chunks, slash through
the catsmeat, fill up the soup pot, fill up the flat
with smells of cooking, smells of burning, when one can

read no more books, write nothing again—this is
a spent legacy, the end of a fine tradition
and a way of keeping the hope alive in hands

that might otherwise turn to murder or to rape
acquire a tic, fall to gestures foolish or obscene
or lie limp for hours, palms up, backs resting on the floor.

FINE DEFINITIONS

The things one buys on holidays
to answer a need or satisfy
a passing whim, such as a 3-pack
of polyester pants, a gaudy towel
a novel or a pair

of blue sunglasses: then coming out
of the dark shop dangling
one's purchases self-consciously
the dazzling sun
catches one unawares

as the lurking photographer
his composition of clichés. Fine
definitions of the self! For years
one comes across them stuffed
unopened at the back of drawers

a puzzle to oneself and to one's heirs.

AMONG THE RUINS

1 In Padua

We got out when the train stopped
between Verona and Venice.
Sunday afternoon: not the best time
to arrive in any Italian city:
in Padua, not the best.
I remember the Byzantine
domes of Saint Anthony, a slick
of green canal under a wall
its mosquitoes feeding
upon us and a clock
counting each hour twice:
it seemed right
for such a careful city, obsessed
with medicine, the law,
and the recovery of lost property
but kept us awake all night.

And next morning, such heat!
only the padrona's smile was cold,
a lacquered cabinet of gold fillings
Venetian in its display.
Was it our luggage she disliked
our northern gaucheness, our ungainly
wish to be away?

But later, your soul found a chapel
of blueness and stars
to float the whole morning in
and mine the perfect seashell
of the old anatomy theatre

where I made notes on Harvey
and the hidden motion of the heart
and the circulation, Italian too
for traffic, which brought us round
to Saint Anthony and his golden relics:
a whole life on display. This time though
among the thank offerings for things found
it was our turn to be cold, unaware
of anything we too might lose:
your shoulder bag, the body's fabric
or the way to anywhere.

And so, all afternoon
in a small purgatorial tour
heat and a misread map
kept returning us to the gate
of the green medicinal garden,
Europe's oldest, and locked
against us all afternoon:
our lesson in obedience
to time and its traffic,
and the irregular heart's beat.

Three days of that
sent us back to Verona
where the river ran swift and shallow
and everything seemed more open
love easier, and the heat
just tipped with autumn frost.

Yet Padua is what I remember best
and its hours of hesitation
between heat and shade

and, if I knew the words
I would pray to this lacquered saint
curator of things lost
to keep these, where they were most mislaid.

2 Loch Ewe

After the evening calm, the wind
gets up again. The rusting bell buoy
clanks for lost convoys. A blackness
runs up into the long arms of the hills.

Tomorrow will be calm again, the frosted mountains
majestical as prophets in the crofter's Sabbath.
Under low beams we lie close. A year from now
at the tide's turn, the bell will clank for you also.

3 Val di Chiana

Do you remember
remember
the oak leaves
the thunder?

The sun's slow wheel
from hill to hill
the river crawling
the earth-red wine?

Remember battlements
with ghostly swallows
coming and going
above the café's

iron tables
and grim cardplayers
in hard black hats
through velvet evenings?

Remember lightning
blue all night
over wooded hills:
how can you forget

the hands, pulling
us earthward
the mosquitoes shrilling
and oak leaves under?

O remember remember
Val di Chiana
the green oak leaves
the nights of thunder.

4 Sydney

The ferry rail
asphalt
steel of the Bridge
in this city everything
burns the hand.

The solid geometry
of insurance buildings
wavers and melts
in lagoons of blue fire.

White triangular
flakes of ash
swerve and whirl
before the firestorm.

The heat of things
runs up the arm
finding a heart
of blackened paper.

How can we learn
to live here, love
except as flames
that pass through, dancing?

5 *A Country Hard to Imagine*

'The pilgrims on their way to consult Apollo
used to land at a port called Crisa (Itea now)
and make their slow way up the green ravine
to the mountain's heady air and Apollo's temple.'

That was the third declension in my Greek primer
and already the words looked sexy in their black letters:
THEOROS, THEORIA, theory—about the same time
you were learning them, in a country hard to imagine.

Years after that, the two of us came to Itea
on a hot ferry, rocking in a stink of diesel,
black letters, among other things, having brought us together.

The road was stony, and the oracle told us nothing.
Afterwards we sat on a terrace and looked at the moon.
The letters would tell us everything, if we could read them.

6 In the Third Person

From plain to mountain air, from Trasimene up
to cool Cortona the road climbed
a Dantean switchback, leaving far below
the world of history to sweat, kick and die
in sunstruck bronze: the damned disposing
their limbs by a lake of pitch where sails
distant, moved, and were lost
in sudden flurries of dust. Up here, the town was empty:
Cortona on a Sunday afternoon. A few
rapt souls were whiling out their time:
one slept full length on a wall, under
an oleander tree, another
lectured his girl on 14th century art
first in the museum, then in the empty church.
Then there were ourselves, freed as we supposed
from such demands of time and place, exempt
from history. Did our eyes acknowledge it? I hope so
but can't remember any words we spoke
though they might have been the last that were our own.

That's nonsense, of course: there were years ahead of us,
ages of silver and plain dealing, but it's hard
to accept as fair the rules we only learn
when the game's already lost. 'Someone should have told us'
we grumble (never: 'we should have listened')
not seeing for what they are those tragic gestures
so expressive of ourselves—wine glasses
ritually shattered in last night's grate, a ring
hurled from a cliff, a note left in the dawn,
the whole bad authentic movie with its trains
and tantrums—as just so many knots

in a texture of other lives. What deeds
did our eyes sign away then, what words
spoken to blossom only now,
years later, by a southern ocean
among strangers, among kin, and in lives
which are their own? It's hard for lovers of the self
to settle for immortality on such terms:
to watch as, day by day, their darling
doubles of the mirror become ancestral
photographs, staring outwards from their frame
into a settled future of nondescript names
and dull flotsam of family history,
the faded he and she of anecdote.
The sun shines here too, by the ebbing water
encircling a head in which its music moves;
a child squats in the grass, peers through a green tunnel
down long afternoons of summer
and summer upon summer. Oh hold back time,
show us our true selves again!

At Cortona, church and museum closed, the lecturer
fell into silence, the sleeper woke
and forgot his dream. A car
started up in the piazza and drove down
into night shadowing the plain and historic lake:
from the momentary heights of you and me
into the common ground of he and she and it.

I saw today exuberantly flower
a rhododendron tree which might have been you:
your voice sang from its vermilion fire.

That is how we become music, history:
a tangle of weed and branches and two
dead birds drifting seaward
caught in the sun-reflecting tide.

AN OBLIQUE VIEW

>   *for Russell & Fiona Poole*

Hills were always elsewhere, lost
in the blues of childhood or
waiting in a shadowy future to

gather one to their breasts, but
in this city of the plain
buildings were what was real. There they stood

like our disgruntled schoolmasters
stranded by the tide of war
in pools of the quotidian but sighing for

a lost glamour: the T&G
clocktower, the phthisic spire
of the RC church facing that stubbier

gothic horror the Wesleyan
chapel where sermons were dosed
out by the hour: brown varnish in spoons and

Death plaqued upon brick walls.
Useful though to have standards
to measure The Beautiful by, and ones which

last me still, so I've never
been able since to live on a
plain, write prose, or care for those unstructured

areas which need the planner's
geometry to make them feel
like home: I'm not political, but don't there-

fore deny its tribute to
the brave art deco of the clock
tower, especially when, as today

its cream is backed by purple
thunderclouds: a mark to find
one's bearings, whether from low *Bunnythorpe*

or vacant *Ashhurst*, dozing in
its Sabbath under the hills
so near the escape routes to capes of morning

or the volcanic North. Aber
die anderen, die Blauen!
Ruahines, presences at the end

of the long melancholy
streets with their nondescript names:
Featherstone, Fitzherbert, Grey, or your own

Ferguson—whom did those names
commemorate? No doubt
their works lay all about us, but it was

the hills which gave assurance
to our dreams of sex, the lame
trickle of that new substance, not the prose

of sermons or of letters to
the editor, but a quite
different matter, one to make a world from.

It was goodbye then to towers
of regret, squares of discontent:
from the hills to us a river ran in

bold curves of promise, its un-
stopped gossip filling our days
with a whole lexicon for the Elsewhere

the Now where hawks hang in the blue
and tributaries burrow down
through clays beginning their long journey to

the sea: water and earth
stamped with the words of praise. How
appropriate then to recover them

in such serious company:
guardians of language who know
that words are all we have to travel by

passing us out from boredom
and helping to give shape to
discomforts not even they can take away

until at last they leave us
in the ocean of aphasia.
Take, then, these mannered ones of gratitude

for kindness that prompted them:
an embrace, talk under trees,
and, from an upstairs window, an oblique view.

THE COMPASS POINTS NORTH

for Keith Macleod

Poems presenting themselves as summons: a cold grip
around the bowels halfway across the piazza
between church and campanile, just when you'd planned
the day like a Victorian traveller's, instructive
yet enjoyable in its slices of sun and shade
gliding from church to church, iced coffee at mid-morning
and the fat blue notebook filling: then, beyond the lagoon,
the northern world of marriage and commerce waiting
to unroll itself without surprises—

        old ladies too
experience such summons, the need, poor things
to find the right container: packed with certificates
and specimens of merit the cardboard boxes
pile up under the bed in strata, waiting in hope
for naturalists with lavender gloves to classify
God's evidence of lives that seemed, at breathless times
to point beyond themselves—

        but look, the cameras
are rolling already, homing in on you
as you hurry back at mid-morning, a time
that will always seem just wrong, to a disordered flat
the body of a stranger, and a mad need
for suitcases, tickets, tweedy disguises, flight
over northern moors, down tumbled stream beds,
a fishing hotel at evening, and the final hazard
slipping quietly under the grey waters of the loch
coffined in steel—

The Entrance to Purgatory

                That's all to come. Meanwhile
hunched in a darkening room, you turn the leaves
more blank than written on, of a stranger's diary
containing an address, your own, a list of precepts
numbered and highlighted in fluorescent gold
for a beloved son, and, most puzzling of all
a sequence of weather reports—

                                  Nothing means
what it appears to mean, yet in the end
decipherment may be child's play, the cryptogram
asking only to be uttered, but as yet too wise for you.
Great simplicity is called for, if minds
are to meet at all, if there is to be love, if deaths
are to be managed. Buried in all this
is a time, and a location, yours,

                                        or yours, Victorian traveller
stayed by typhoid in a famous city,
old lady bedridden upon memories, spy,
and fugitive with a burden. Working in haste
using such analects as you can find
you plot the advance of a front across the map
its isograms decoding to the shape
of a future you had no claim to, a language of the heart
you have yet to learn: to see, if only for a moment
the way that he or she would move on hills
through shafts of sun and rain, renewed in season.

THE ENTRANCE TO PURGATORY

What you will notice first is the air's
greater clarity: you had not remembered
how it gave to trees the instructive simplicity
of a botanist's drawing. The hills too, so distant
but so sharply delineated, seeming to wait
for a turret, a temple, a whole town
circumscribed by justice: in the foreground a space
left for Madonna and Infant, and in the southern sky
new stars hanging as beacons of virtue.

You are glad to be here, when it would have been so easy
at the last moment simply to permit
the past its habitual choice: blind, heavy-handed
and hopeless in its passion. Even so
that you are here, that you are no longer hunting
an imaginary shape through streets of lead
turning back always upon the same dead vista
of northern cities which have lost their hearts for ever
seems mere chance, although it is not.

For the light which bathes these streets is sober, the sun
though welcoming as love is placed to illuminate
an architecture whose details always tell
the same legend. Those whiskered bigots who planned
this city in holy ignorance of its terrain
meant it a cradle of virtue, but perhaps you must
return here more than once, your suitcase crammed
with disappointments and leading loss by the hand
to learn how insistently its ways will bring

The Entrance to Purgatory

you always to one point, until their choice becomes
your second nature. But this is only the beginning
when suffering seems a new adventure, the past
a backdrop lending it dignity. Later you must unpack
pictures and broken ornaments, making them
the measure of your loss, and what it takes to forgive.
Here too the city will help, hill tree and tower
by sunlight or by starlight assembled into a setting
for something to take place in, a place to go on from.

IX ∾ The Heart's Hard Edge

Each day a new horizon
swelling under the heart's hard edge.

—'A Late Honeymoon'

A LATE HONEYMOON

   1 Voiles

We are wearing exactly the clothes
for such summer expeditions—
practical, worn to dullness, confining:
the hats against the sun, the laced boots for walking,
our broadcloth statements about Nature.

Standing here, a little separate
the rough ground of rocks and bushes between
we see the sea's blueness framed
by two grotesque pinnacles,
chalk at this distance glinting like ice

but ready to crumble obediently
under the master touch of winter rains.
Returning, we shall draw closer
on the downward path to the hotel
where white curtains billow by an open window.

We do not speak at all
feeling no need for conversation:
the afternoon holds us in its golden arms.
Tonight I shall write in my diary:
'Walked to clifftop with H. Fine view of sea.'

Such fantastic shapes the rain carves!
But you can't beat the sea for simplicity
and the statements of flat calm.
Look: far out, a breeze has caught two tiny sails
and draws them steadily to the white horizon.

[September 1985]

2 *Nuages*

Clouds do not move.
Our world travels eastward
mole, lighthouse, priory
under the Alps of night.

These huge golden calthrops
one foot on the particular
invite us to sleep and dream.

We were such travellers!
Each day a new horizon
swelling under the heart's hard edge.

Here are we narrowly lodged:
too early each new night gathers
over the still furrowed bed.

The books rest heavy on the windowsill.
Beside them, a drying shell
sheds its hoarded sand.

The North Sea could not be calmer.
We are lovers of the infinite:
our bodies expand to clouds.

[19 October 1985]

3 *Brouillards*

The years that were wasted, the years
that you could only imagine
feeling them swell inside you, like the breath
a child holds, counting round-eyed
the seconds up to sixty—

all these have gone. See how they drift
over the city, through
the pine plantation and the grey
grass of the dunes, and out to sea.

Tomorrow is full of a light that pierces:
gulls with their stabbing cries and the tiny
boats with masts like yellow needles
rocking crazily.

[MS-4150/006, variant MS-2674/185, MS-4150/004, MS-4150/009]

VOICES

Long after the sun had gone
three poets sat on, talking.

The first said:
though not a religious man
I see that wrong we do ourselves
and the earth, sometimes righted by a natural good.
What else is there worth speaking of?

The second said:
though not a religious man
I hear sometimes voices penned in things
claim utterance such as makes the light
ripple out eastward over folded hills.

The third said:
though not a religious man
I think that if I shouted loud enough
the sound would not travel out forever
but find some foreign shore to break against.

And darkness fell
in its silent wave upon
all choices right and wrong;
upon the cities and the hills
silence upon silence.

[MS-4150/004]

SLOW GLASS

   for Ann

The river is flowing backwards.
We wander down it to its source
picking up leaves and dead twigs
and throwing them away.
The sky is brown, always brown
it is late autumn or winter
someone's dog frisks, a child is running backwards.

I installed this window four years ago:
the landscape begins to come slowly through.
Not everything is clear but, from this distance
we appear to be in love, certainly content
and even happy. We are taking
an afternoon walk along a river

    under the brown sky of winter

a child, and the river, running backwards.

[November 1985, AS, MS-2674/185, variant MS-4150/004]

TARAWERA, LAKE & MOUNTAIN

to Ann

Look, we can make miracles:
from the end of the jetty
you are walking towards me
steadily out of your photograph

cleared every minute

the lake's glass unlocked by the wind
flows easily as love
into an assured future.

Why then do we keep these visions
of plateaux and slopes of ash
where nothing will ever grow
and the past is locked forever
into this volcanic shape
beautiful and unforgiving?

[6 January 1986, AS]

JOURNEY NORTH

1

I want to remember, now
while it's happening, how
easy it seemed and natural
how
like a cliché the road
snaking toward us and the wheel

shuddering under my hands   now
while it's still happening and
(Timaru)
the sea curdled by the wind
to a warm yellow milk
reading your letter yet again
(Canterbury Norwester)
even faster because of the heat and
(now)
the first intimation
a new law   the attraction
increases inversely to the distance
(faster)
because of the heat and
I've taken my shirt off
and put it on Love
(and we're really racing)

   2

Amberley
beach the slow
surf flops on fine
grey shingle the last
sun catches the headland
a tentroof flaps
in the dying wind
at dawn a patter
of rain

3

Kooked Kaikoura Krayfish 2
tunnels through the rock
the sea the sea the garageman's
wife still rubbing her puffy
eyes (was it love? was it booze?
or just
midsummer madness?)
tea and scones we might even
make it to Picton up and down
into Marlborough the hot noon
Sunday heady with hops the sky
like a blue cathedral
(now!)
while it's still happening
now
'I simply waved
this plastic thing at him
like a magic sword
and he waved me on
through this vast iron door thing'
(and now)

4

there are 200 fathoms beneath us
and our car and the sea
is calm and is blue and it seems
that someone made a decision
somewhere back there

and anyway we can't go back
now
(now!)

5

Waikanae
Kapiti
It's New
Year's Day and so
early there's nobody
on the road it's our
road
Otaki
Foxton
I lived
here when I was a kid I remember
these pines and sandhills
I love them so early
There's no-one about
Himatangi
Sanson
on bikerides
with sandwiches
and I'd never
it's early
it's our road
any faster
and I'll fly
Mangakino
Utiku
I remember so well
I'm flying back
definitely
there's something
at the other end of the string
(there always was)

6

the road climbs
through clays by moonlit
cliffs where trees
hang shadows the iron
girders of bridges
crisscross glimpsed
in moonlight through steamed
windows of trains
(o once, in another—
o hush my love
and sleep again)

the road climbs
back into slow
motion now   time drags
at our heels
in a dream
in a dream
(o once
o hush)
no time
to remember
no time

7

the desert
   the mountain
travels serenely
   as fast as us
however fast

the mountain the lake
as fast as us
(and last week killed
a boy of twelve)

   8

I want to remember, now
while it's happening easily
as a movie cliché   I want
to remember now because later
there won't be time
to remember and it will never
be better and it will never
be better than now I'm turning
the last corner   the speed   the attraction
increasing inversely   baby this blue
car is really *flying*
'o god' you said, and
'a yellow skirt'
and we've never actually *met*
(and they never actually met)
and now
and now
remember
remember

[28 January 1986, AS, variant MS-2674/185, MS-4150/004]

'DEAR ANN, THIS PRESENT I ENCLOSE'

Dear Ann, this present I enclose
Says something of my feeling too,
Viz: pragmatism's just a pose.

My thoughts are all concerned with you
And (though it's risky to disclose)
My heart insists on being true.

I read, make cups of tea, and doze,
Find time a drag when lacking you
And pragmatism just a pose

My wits anomalous and askew
That for a minute could suppose
My heart be anything but true.

I wonder how your garden grows—
I cultivate my garden, too
But pragmatism's still a pose—

I might have known it wouldn't do.
The future's murky, but who knows?
If hearts insist on being true

And birthdays still may bring us close
I hope you'll write and tell me you
Find pragmatism just a pose
And what I feel, you're feeling too:
Your heart insists on being true.

[AS, variant MS-4150/006]

NOT A POEM

I haven't yet written you a love poem—
not the kind you'd like: something direct
a straightforward celebration
of small moments—at the airport say
parting or meeting, a walk
under autumn trees or along a beach
last night's passion
facing this morning's coolness—all simple
as folksong in its pleasure and pain.
Well I can't do it. The moment I try
the big bass notes come throbbing in
like clumsy blowflies, with boring ostinatos
of love and death, the wry counterpoint
of interrogation, and I find I need a string quartet
and centuries of civil culture
not to speak of philosophy and foreign languages.
Well, that's a difference between us
and another awkward element to be worked into the music
    somehow
and so I give up. I'd like to be direct
and I've a whole headful of moments, stones and shells
each too individual to describe
and far too valuable to throw away.
I can't make necklaces or bracelets from them
and they worry me, sitting there
in the darkness of my skull, with nobody to share them
not even you. So what can I do?
Here's one, for example (and it's not poetry):
our second morning together: two shy people
facing each other boldly in a swimming pool

crowded with strangers we were able to ignore.
It was drizzling, I remember.
You were wearing your blue swimming costume.
I didn't mind your looking at me.

[AS, variant MS-4150/004]

LE GRAND MEAULNES

That spring when we read
Le Grand Meaulnes
absorbed into it
as if into our own lives
the morning sun releasing
the white lace balcony
would move around to fill
the wax-scented dining room
with golden dust-motes.
Between morning and afternoon
a whole year would pass:
later I see us facing
down the leaf-filled track
that led to the memorial gate
with mud churned around it.

Today I find myself reading
our life together
as if it were *Le Grand Meaulnes*
and we trapped inside it
like dust motes in a sun filled room
moving around with the seasons.

[8 June 1986, MS-3619/043]

WATCHING WAR FILMS

The blue-grey canister
sinking through blue-green
depths until buoyed
by its own weight of
water suddenly
erupts : heraldic
shockhead of water spears, pure
white, balanced, then falling out
by numbers into the still
heaving blue—

with what fine
tuning of hands
to load the charge
and turn the fuse key
we convoy our private wars
into public domains, the seas
of epic, arctic white
or aegean blue—

but the art remains
beyond us, un-
biddable: there may /
may not be something around
to decide what shall be relevant:
to notice a bowed
head dribbling tears
over experienced hands
and see in a flash how epics
must begin, and end, in supplication.

[13 September 1986, MS-4150/004]

BY DEFINITION

The Greeks had a word for it
meaning the right time
iron hot, the opportunity
golden, and meaning too
'content', as in
a mortal wound or blow.

By definition
what happened to you
must have been at the right time:
it was something you could *know*.

But what *you* did
—leaving on a journey
consulting an oracle
or choosing to die
not necessarily so.

[MS-4150/004]

LETTER IN DECEMBER

I've just hung the print I discovered
in the Public Library: two
lovers painted by some member
of the Swabian school, hands joined
around an unidentifiable plant
wearing identical rings. Each looks
slightly confident, as if
they'd made a desirable marriage.
It's probably not Northern: you

would have liked it.
On the turntable
this black disc smoothly revolves
by the arcane mechanics of time which makes possible
the ebb and flow of Victoria's great Mass.
Between the speakers, your loved Victorian sideboard
with its elegant moving top: behind it
three years and a hemisphere away
I can just see the curve of your cheek.
The house is full
of objects chosen carefully
to represent occasions quite other
than those of thought: like the suit
you chose one calm September evening
for me to wear at your funeral
on a December evening cold enough
to cut the heads off flowers.
I'm wondering
for what future occasions
I'm choosing things now.
Those lovers in the painting—
are they ourselves? If you'd seen it
you would have wanted it
as you wanted the Universe
for what it said about ourselves,
what no thing could? What do they know
about us? Is it why they're smiling?
And Victoria's Kyrie
that seems still to hover above your bed
the blue folds hanging straight to the ground.
What is it trying to say?
There's some strained and attenuated sense

in which you're here: simple enough
when I don't think about it too long.
I've arranged things here
not as if you might need them
but as if some part of you still clung
to each of them: together, they make the ground
for you being here. Look, I'm losing you
and you're beginning to slip away.
Stay with me, at least
till the music's ended: it's travelled
all that way from its century like light
to be with us tonight, like the pair
in the painting who are surely ourselves.

[MS-4150/004]

REFLETS DANS L'EAU

It was as if they were dreaming:
the bridge, with its much painted light;
at their feet, repeated in the river's oils
the play was about to begin.

Holding hands, they faced
in opposed directions; the curtain rose
the curtain rose.
It was as if they were dreaming.

The music swirled in blended
chords around the piers.
Light pointed at the buildings:
the play was about to begin.

The curtain rose, and there
were the lovers in their costumes.
The play was about to begin.
It was as if they were dreaming.

[MS-4150/004]

AT LEAST

A frost last night
    So no wind today
At every now
    A quiet stir
A leaf detaches
    And circles grassward
In the crisp air
    Yet how golden still!
Who at the end
    Fails to find
Autumn best
    Of all love's seasons?
In your letter too
    A band of blue light
Scissored sharply
    Between beginning and end
Something nipped off
    Between *dear* and *love*
Not to grow again
    Though next season but one
A new leaf
    For the tree at least

[MS-4150/009]

X ∾ Winter Walk at Morning (1991)

To souls
no definite place is granted.

—'The Winter Walk at Morning'

ODYSSEUS IN TRAVELLAND

The trees swept scarlet to the water's edge:
Reaching up from his lilo he could pluck
Their golden nameless fruit. Snorkelling
Far out over the reef he could see
Blue fish with yellow spots. Certainly
The island offered all that EPICTRAVEL said.

So why these tears on the shore, these thin
Quarrels and hump-backed evasions of love?
Why couldn't he be happy? Penelope
Was surely dead by now, and Calypso, though celtically
Fey, marked by the sun's cocked hat upon her skin
Where the atolls of felicity begin.

Didn't he know Calypso was a device
Invented by the Poet to keep him back
Seven years while Telemachus grew up?
—Himself the helpless arrow of his plot
Notched in the bowstring and aimed straight at
Next year's Olympicorp Poetry Prize?

All happiness is in the mind, the Riddler said
(Another figure from the inexhaustible world
Of art and islands). Behind Calypso's veil
Was just another veil, Penelope's farewell
Best of a dozen sexy poses. Back to
Olympus the Muse of Pragmatism sped

Concerned about her shares and a collapse
In the market, leaving our hero neutralised
Between dream and a specious magic. Let's leave him too
Mooching along the beach. The holiday
Is drawing to its end. Soon he'll step out
From travel agent's literature—into life perhaps?

PHILEMON AND BAUCIS

They lived with great contentment in an ad
For life insurance, gliding smooth between
The blue retirement village sky, the green
Of cemetery lawns. All that they had

Was all they'd ever asked, and not too bad
At that, when others soaked themselves unseen
Behind blinds, lived on pet food, grew unclean
Mismanaged their annuities, went mad.

Circling like veteran dancers who stare through
Invisible panes beyond each other's eyes
Displaying gaiety in a waxen smile

Was a skill they'd dearly learned, and they were wise
To practise it, since that was what they knew.
The dance would finish in a little while.

DEAD RECKONING

At the class in navigation we were warned
By cheerful captain Parry (who'd retired
From trundling tankers up and down the Gulf,
To take this shore job while in mid career,
Having 2 children and a charming wife)
How much depends on seeing that the ship's
Chronometers are *regularly* wound.
You need your GMT to work a fix:
To forget to wind them was a heinous crime
Injurious to young officers' careers.

'Captain' was purely honorific, like
'Doctor' or 'Professor', though he held
His master's ticket. When he left the trade
They'd offered a command which he turned down
With no regrets. He told us that he never
Read books about the sea, not since he'd swopped
Norie's Tables for *Christie's Glasshouse Guide*.
Meeting him one lunchtime in the street
Outside John Edmonds, *Ironmongers &*
Hardware Merchants since 1888,
I saw that he was carrying a pair
Of edging shears. He gave a courteous smile.
A fellow student turned to me and said
'I forgot to wind them once.' We shared a desk,
Dividers, an outdated almanac:
Much older than the rest, he took the course
For interest, he said, and meant for lack
Of any better way to spend his evenings
Now that his wife was dead, and kids away,
And it was something he'd once learned to do
Though never well, and had forgotten since.
'The Old Man found out of course, and didn't he
Give me a bollocking. It was Christmas Eve
And snowing wet and we were going down
The London River. I was feeling low,
Sailing like that on Christmas Eve, instead
Of spending it at home. Perhaps that was why
I forgot to wind the buggers. Anyhow
I never forgot again.' We both turned back
To the next problem: 'August 26.

D.R. position 52°
And 16' N, 7°
And 30' E. The altitude
By sextant of the star Arcturus was
10 and 15.2'
Ship's time was 1930 GMT
10h.13m.25
s. Find the information needed
To lay off your position line.' We did.

CAMBRIDGE IN THE FIFTIES

1 11.30 from Liverpool Street

In the dim light of the smoking compartment
the black USAF sergeant, returning

to base through 'flu-ridden fenlands, entertained
2 corporals with a story of a house in

Camden and what he'd done there to the girl who
wouldn't, as he put it, do fuck with him.

The carriage juddered, made a drainpipe smell.
Sprawling under the lamp they yawned, scratched balls:

3 of them, ignoring the 2 of us, cowed
to a shared silence, much as they ignored

the buttoned upholstery, the blackened country
outside and its history of

Saxon invaders nosing their craft up creeks.
What is home, I wondered, and do we need it?

returning to mine and feeling 'flu coming
on, like chemical fog over the marshes.

2 *In the Mill Lane Lecture Rooms*

Deferring to our greying tutors (younger
now than ourselves) we took 'au pied

de la lettre' as we mincingly put it their
languid advice to attend F.'s lectures if

we 'thought we could afford the time'.
                                        Upstaging
the dais with its NO SMOKING sign he spoke

gownless and without notes on topics Cambridge
had never examined, one hand deep in

the pocket of his loose American tweed
jacket, gesturing sharply with the other,

his accent one we'd learned mostly from sitting
in the smoky pits of provincial cinemas

on wet Wednesday afternoons.
                              Toadying
to a system already half-dismantled before

we arrived in it, we hid concern
behind the smile learned in our first week, and carefully

avoided taking notes.
                      But all of us were losers.
Thirty years after, hearing of his death

I remember the hand deep in the pocket,
nonchalance dissembling not just good looks

but a life stepped out of like a movie set
remote as Tibet or Hitler's Germany

from our unease.
                                 The image
snags briefly, then jerks forward again and leaves

only a slight tear.

LINES ON A PHOTOGRAPH

The wind (there's always wind
on this headland) flattens the tussock, makes
the sea's blue bluer even
than your camera could catch it. Still
it's your best photograph to date.
The tussock's golden, flattening
to yellow in the wind, sometimes
to brown. It's like hair.
I'm quite small:
in my red shirt and blue trousers
and what could be a gun in my arms
I'm a small tin soldier standing
in the middle of your photograph.
It's all I know how to do.
If the wind blows any harder
it'll take me with it, melting me
into all that blue.
I'm only a part, but I'm at the centre.
Without me it wouldn't be a photograph.

EXILE

> *for Bill Sewell*

The air will do something to our skin: burn it
and make us young again. We have arrived
and deployed along the lakeshore a variety of things
each with its special use. The slender children
with special needs poise on the edge of boredom
like archaic statues, inscribing with one toe
a question in the sand. How blue the sky
how green the forest! The light of paradise
makes every leaf particular: the number of things
in the world is finite, and each one of us
has his god-given talent. The great cliffs smile down
and guarantee our happiness.

                        Guidebooks describe
the water here as 'pristine': that means free
from imported sludges, but the headland hides
a burial ground where dark roots twist among bones
assembled from three continents. Anyone who arrives
may claim this as his own: two women
who got here first now furiously repack
their rusted Campavan, but the waves
of immigration beating upon the shore
can't be stopped: already an armada
of powerboats is drawn up along the beach
sharp prows in the air. The air is loud
with transistorised warcries: before the day is out
a head will be bloodied on black obsidian.

Noon shimmers, and a smoke of cooking curls
along the shore. The Brownian motion

of human particles is stilled by an artist
recording it at her easel. We shall be viewed
in the halls of some mid-century exhibition
picturesque and anonymous at our point of passage.

Someone calls for sausages. Grasping a spear
a sharkskinned diver lectures his gaping audience
on the typology of tits. This is exile—
being among people one will never understand
however smooth the trunks of trees, renewed
endlessly in the green water, however blue the sky.

Over there on the sand that pale-skinned couple
regard us attentively, as if we might have met
in another country, and exchanged words
heavy with the silt of meaning. But look:
the sun dips and the lake is waiting for us:
where are the thorns on which we must hang our skins?

[26 April 1986]

ANCESTRAL GROUND

These places that seem half factory, half—what?
—spacious like power houses, glassed clear
leaving no corner for misery to breed:
an abstract structuring of space whereby
wise authority accommodates our loss:
one curtain wall, clad in cheerful brick
suspends a slim and lightly varnished cross
dividing us from the room next door—that window too high
to see through ever—gravel swept bare
to its concrete base: stations tended with municipal care.

Winter Walk at Morning

This one's different only by being perched
on the land's edge. You could look miles away
from the blonded oak, out where the sea
slides smoothly in, its silken rollers
a faint blue-grey; or, if it's spring
to the gorse that blossoms gold along the cliffs;
and think if you like of hats and dresses
or the colour of eyes or of anything
but these decent faces turned lumpy with tears
and hands knotting on the backs of chairs.

Outside in the carpark the assembled rows
of cars are waiting, each different and all the same,
to drive away soon; and beyond the cars, the same
grey slabs repeated in orderly rows.
There's a quiet rumbling somewhere, as though
a river fell through turbines far below.
Activity interrupted: a ladder against a wall:
someone's been painting the roof, gone home for lunch
or out of respect, and will be back again soon
to brush and whistle all through the afternoon.

Inside we wait for what can never occur,
changes our lives for ever, but passing gives no sign.
What happens, happens elsewhere: underground, within;
yet goes on happening as long as waves come rumbling in.
I think most of our poverty that contrives
such poor space to unvest ourselves of lives:
heads bent in shame, hands that unknot and unbutton
and knot up again to go out and on:
all caught in the homely legend that turns around
this abstract space, our one ancestral ground.

[December 1985]

FOLK MEMORY

You planted cemeteries on slopes
because the soil drained well
to the swamp below
and not for the view—

a modern fancy, that.
Sheeted in taut doctrine
and laid in coffins
to wait for resurrection

they expected to see nothing
of what passed between:
survivors bringing flowers
and dying in their turn

before the century was out.
In 1898 this one
BORN IN COUNTY GALWAY
at 53. Compute that.

Though they did build here
in part for the view:
a bay, dark green hills
and the rain clouds like home.

The swamp's a sportsground
but floods after rain.
Viewed by gasometers
light industry filled the flats.

Changes in land use:
great grandchildren playing
among the plots, paint-spray
what they can't overturn.

Who's to care? Memory's short
if you're born with no view.
Punched cans, plastic bags
brighten the enclosures:

too much space, perhaps
in a home away from home
or need for the proper place
to sanctify action.

The generations meet here
with no word to say.
The Oval's sheeted with water
reflecting a blank sky.

MIRROR LANGUAGE

We can't go on meeting like this
or in this place: the dark
acrid hotel corridor
with its mirror at the far end

never knowing whether this time
it's to be farce or melodrama: who
will I see in the mirror, Groucho
or the woman in white?

I say: it must end sometime, I
have a life to get on with, but you—
and as soon as I say it, lip read
the mirror's answer in mirror language

complaining 'what would I do all day?
There's nowhere to go: it's so boring here
and besides
you couldn't get on without me.'

Oh mirror language is so banal
and everything it says is true:
with us, it can never be
tragedy or comedy: we pad

the length of the commonplace
like a carpet damp underfoot
and turn and pad back again
but do we want to be free?

Why, as soon as I suggest it, the
tinnitus of nightmare begins
the pursuit through silence and dark: 'how
can I live

if you hide yourself from me?'
to the meeting at some nowhere
with your pale-lipped reproach: 'why
did you kill my love dead?'—fictions

which leave us with nothing to invent.
We need each other, as the themes
of tragedy need each other:
love facing death in the mirror.

A SUMMER AT PURAKANUI

Something in us too is ground
down all the time that can never
be made up again: look at these coarse

grains separate in the hand
that were held together in the kinship
of rock that lasts for ages—

                      look at the blackened
sticks of kelp and the bleached
broom twigs and the dirtied
wing of the gull
half covered in grey sand
and fluttered by the wind—

listen to the wind whisper
listen to the sea—
you'll hear a kind of cosmic breathing
in and out
then in and out again.
It too could dry up
and there be nothing: hard
for us to understand
who find this all too easy

the grinding of rock to sand
our walking away and saying nothing.

[29 May 1986]

CALIBAN AT THE TYPEWRITER

Actually I find it much easier
than holding a pen, somewhat too slender
for my cloven paws, and then my fur
tends to smudge the ink. And wasn't there something
about monkeys and typewriters? Strange reversal,

the Creature writing the Author's Works.
Prospero's away, leaving his typewriter unlocked:
he taught me language, but he doesn't know
that art is aleatory. That's my modern discovery:
listen: the air is full
of electronic music and this whole
round island's just a Happening. However:
that's not what I wanted to tell you—
my thumping the keys has a more serious purpose.
You shouldn't believe the yarns
that sailors tell of me. I don't smell of fish.
I can carry my drink
like a gentleman, and I know
a *real* god when I see one.
Actually, I am six feet tall. The penguins hereabouts
tell me I look well in tails: I'm the life and soul
of the Seawrack Nitespot. My foxtrot
is really something to be seen. Personally
I've always believed I am a throwback
to the Scott Fitzgerald generation. I feel
a profound kinship with Gatsby: I'm the last
romantic. I number Polyphemus
among my ancestors: like him, I'm good-hearted
with a rough sense of humour, and a born loser:
all I ever really wanted
was a few sheep and a Galatea
to keep me company.
But I've had my admirers: 'You should be more ambitious'
they say, and 'Why don't you write a book?'
Nobody could accuse me of vanity. I've known
some quite famous poets, among them

Mr B and Mr A. The latter
discerned something of my true nature
and made me talk like Henry James: language
is my real forte. My detractors will tell you
that I can't string three words together
but just listen to me now. After all,
I had the best of teachers.

But you really ought to see me foxtrot.

[November 1985]

WAKING UP IN NAPLES

Oranges were ripening all along the tracks
in early February. It was hot and blue as Africa.
Hannibal's elephants coming the long way round
must have taken years longer until they swayed
carefully down the passes like elderly tourists.
Our white Italian liner smoked mildly in the Bay
between two beauties from the NATO fleet
spreading their delicate antennae in the sun.
The stewards shooed us gently ashore
down passageways piled with Alps of bed linen
feet slithering in the red Campanian mud.

The world was so dirty and so white! Our pensione
smelt of sauce and urine, and in the *gabinetto*
was a plastic basket stuffed with crumpled paper:
whose job was it to empty it, I wondered:
the cook's? you ventured. Giggling like children
we entered the suicidal liftcage and shuddered earthward.

There was everything to laugh at: Herculaneum, Pompeii
Vesuvius looking pleased with itself, and the rolls
of papyrus burnt to a crisp, along with the philosophers
who wrote them to assure us that death is nothing
if we devote ourselves seriously to pleasure.
We saw the anonymous dead, caught in their sudden movement
by a satirical twist of time, encased
in volcanic mud and looking more like ourselves
than art could have made them. This was Europe,
beginning in Naples and still on the right side of forty.

It was night when we got back to our room, its ornate wardrobe
pinnacled in gloom near the ceiling: 'where
else but in Italy would you *use* a 20 watt bulb?'
You peered up at it, perched carefully over the bidet
smart boots still streaked with Neapolitan mud.
                                                  On the enormous bed
we lay down and died with laughter.

Next morning we found the balcony. You opened
the shutters and sudden sunlight
enclosed you in a golden frame. There was the Bay,
sails imprinted on it like tiny white hands.
The room was transfigured, and packed with fictions
to blur the sharp gaze of time, among them
this painting by Turner, captioned
'The Admiral viewing the city's destruction
from his flagship at Misenum.' I can almost remember
the livid sky and the fireglow repeated
on the gold border of his cloak. Next to it hung
Lady Hamilton as Aurora, rising from her gilded couch

to breakfast with the Ambassador: 'She was all Nature
yet all Art too.'
                              Below us
red tiles of churches slithered down the hill like lava.

[25 October 1985]

NEARLY SO

Good spot for a picnic
you said, where a river
approached the road—2 modes
of travel intersecting, or nearly so.

Far off, the dark hump
of a mountain peered over the edge of a plain big
enough to form, elsewhere, a shire
mark or city state, guarding
its ancient dialect against invasion, leaving
its name in history as byword
for cunning or provincial dullness, its eccentric
national poet one of the famous
headwaters of that great river from which
the least of us draw as it flows
through barbarian wastes, past younger languages.

Unpacked, the four of us, a
family, or nearly so—
yellow tartan rug, blue
thermos, salt cellar, the wicker
basket and child's beaker

with its bumblebee motif, each
anecdotal object arranged
ritually upon the rug, used, repacked
and carried elsewhere, small gods
in search of a household.

The river sang over gravel, black-
backed gulls loafed on shingle piled
by the last flood. Over the further
bank, undercut and crumbling, the mountain peered
curiously.

   White-
ankled paterfamilias I paddled
across just to see if I could
gauge that way, roughly
the flow in cumecs, and now that we'd
stopped to get some sense of
the bigness of the plain, if it could really
swallow a culture like that.
      No sign
of settlement anywhere. Broom and matagouri
colonised earlier channels, the sky
was populated by singing larks. There were
mountains all around, big as giants, one got
a sense of proportion.
     There wasn't much
to the flow, you could never
irrigate the whole plain from it. For all that
it was going somewhere, making something of itself
in a young country. I splashed back
through the shallow braids. One needs

to get a sense of history, as member of
a small nomadic family, or nearly so
picnicking by a young river's babble, learning,
if you listen carefully, its idiolect.

DISTANCES

We pedal abreast, amicably wrangling
up the Highcliff Road. Forty or so
years between us matters less
than the distance we've done, a solid achievement
which you gravely compute. Sun flashes
off chrome and silica, it's
the first day of spring.
                        We dismount
toil up where
the soldier stands on his clump of basalt
facing north, to Belgium I suppose
and 1918, as if the past was always in front of us
the future always at our back
washing over our heads towards an emptiness
from which we can't turn our eyes.

My legs are suddenly ungeared
so I sit for a while, shoving
my back against a basalt outcrop
as if, this way, I could stop the world spinning
headlong. We can hear, not see, a dozen groundlarks
and six hundred feet downhill the rollers
boom in from the south. It takes, I think
about 6 seconds until the muted roar
arrives. Just before they topple, the underside

flashes like blue glass. We can see the breakers
but they haven't quite made it to our world.
The city's back there. Through my telescope
I can just make out our house, and almost
the verandah where I might be reading now.
Is that the past, or is it the future?

                                           At this point you ask me
don't I want to be here? From 13
the question comes disquieting
with its suggestion of a possible emptiness
neither of us might inhabit.
The larksong is suspended, or unheard
while I think how to answer it. Finally
I say I'll settle for both, then close my eyes
pushing against the boulder at my back
with what strength I have. For you
I'd like to fill up all the distances
and make them solid, like basalt.

[14 September 1986, AS]

HOLY LOCH

Out there on the still,
viscid water, even so early
on Easter Sunday, there's a general
coming and going of grey
picket boats, whose half-submerged shapes are gathered
like harpooned whales around the skirts
of a grey mother ship, or stepmother.
Southward again towards the grey
Atlantic, mist peels slowly off the hills

and the sea where last night lights flashed
from *Cloch* and *Gantocks*.
Then the first sun flashes
from a fisherman's oar. There spreads
along the shore smells of seaweed, new baked bread.

On our extravagant excursions each new day
gets lost again in some grey mist.
Today it's *Kilmun*, a hotel window on
the Holy Loch, viscid water
smoke from early fires ascending
and a rare sunlight among
grey latticework of ships.
I came here to resurrect
some fragments of a childhood, small
signifiers accidentally dropped
through layers of green time, banal
and particular, including item: one
penknife in Hong Kong tartan, one retractable
measuring tape spring loaded
in a pink celluloid case, a Morris
8, green and black, stopped halfway up
a glacial valley, ticking cool among heather and mist.
I track each particular down: success
seems unsurprising. It proves nothing.
What was the question? We explore the village
picking our way along the armoured shore,
slow, desultory
sniffing seaweed evocative of something
and laugh at the commentary upon strangers
hooted in Gaelic by a flotilla of geese.
You could call this peace. Why

do we live as if for ever, memory
always failing to warn us
of the winter for which it
hoards so obsessively? Here
is the little church. Against
a wall stands rusting a curious
iron framework or grill. It's meant
to lie flat on new coffins to prevent
resurrection by grave-robbers, a piece
of naive technology, of a piece
with those out in the loch. Death:
not the irony of resurrection.

                              Beside
a drystone wall, a birch beyond it
just delicately coming into leaf, you crouch
in your fashionable overcoat and sketch
the tower. I still have it—
the wall, the tree, the tower, and behind
clear now of mist, the mountains of Argyll.
You left nothing in it to show
what day it was, or century.

[2 November 1986]

TWO PREDICATES

1

How many will read these words—
twenty? Fifty perhaps. A hundred.
Then none.
You, not at all

or in some quite different sense—
the subject of all brave creeds.
So let them go
like the immortal Tom and Jerry
to pirouette upon absurdity—
as well expect the tree
to form again in the swirling leaves
in a dusty sky, a dry autumn.

2

Last night, 20 telephone calls
to America I think, or Australia
or some place beyond that cloud.

In each case, no answer
or wrong number, or the line dead:
who was talking, who listening?

Today, I recall a real telephone box
bobbing upright in the wake of the past
and marking the site of some wreck.

MY TOASTER TELLS THE TIME

One side: time
to read (if you're quick) four
sonnets or intone
one penitential psalm   time
to make a shopping list and feel
a cold or a poem coming on or run
into the great hall of memory and out
again   oh time

to know quite certainly you're
no longer loved that time
is a trickster   time
to fall down dead
and leave time
to grow black and burn
the house with its great hall
its poems lists and lovers that made
the shape and stuff of time.

APRIL THE FIRST

In the flat opposite
a door or window
opens or shuts: someone enters
someone leaves, the world turns over
another autumn begins.
On the table pulled out
from its corner, scrubbed
pushed back again, no trace now
of cup rings, or the ink that flowed
through last summer's passionate letters.
Somewhere behind the eyes
a photograph hangs, and shows
a river up country
impossibly distant snow
the marks water left upon rock.

THE ART OF POETRY

for Kevin

Each morning the cat backs up
to the car's hubcap, lifts her tail
and squirts it deftly. She can't believe
it's the same that occupied
the carport yesterday, still less
the day before. Maybe she's right.
You can't pee on the same wheel twice
said Heraclitus, the plain cat's
philosopher. There's no telling where
a heartfelt wish to keep things fresh
may end. Literary revolutions!
A god, I drive forth on fragrant wheels:
all over the town
a shift in the metrics of cat pee.

KNOWING THE RIGHT PLACES

The name attracted us
Then the guidebook
Promising timbered houses
And coffee at the Angel

On a frosty morning
With not too many about
At that time of year.
All which was true—

And the drive there
Between fields of stubble
Through Lavenham, Long Melford:
Churches with windows,
Clerestory, Clare.

Eighteen years on
I went in summer
With another companion:
'You'll love Clare.'

Air heavy with fennel
By the slow-winding river
Tail-flicking cattle
And the timbered teashop.

To know the right places
Is usually bought dear
And at others' expense.
So we drove there

And found it, again, true:
But the dark timbers
Absorbed sunlight like time
Telling less than they knew

And the prices were higher
In the antique shop
And the past redeemed
Was bogus brassware.

I'd find it sad now
In either season.
I'd go there again, though:
In company, alone.

THE WINTER WALK AT MORNING

Out there where the spilled city began
to crumble at its edges into a spatter of
one-time village names (though any quaint
feature of architecture or sweet natural
touch was now half crusted over or floating in
development, a sort of adaptable
homogeneous flow, vivid like bile)

were first streets without gardens, then with
gardens, creosote-fenced, then allotments
and sheds of iron, though too securely locked
to conceal more than garden tools—so why
should one start to think of raped corpses here, why
should the fluttering loops of surveyor's tape remind
of bloodstained bandages, looped along battlefields?—

dogs, some, perhaps savage. People, no. The time of day,
some TV programme, rush hour, happy hour? No-one.
'Walk, why walk? Nobody goes for walks here.'
Why walk? Either the need
to exercise what whines and snuffles in the heart
walking it out and around, then back again
exhausted, domestic, fit once more to inhabit

cleanly. Or else to recall a memory
of other and earlier walks, their calm patrols
of boundaries, or the heady sense
of voyaging farther out, beyond
*Cold Harbour, The Snares, The Noises, Cape
Desolation*, though it were only a tree
a telephone pole, a dead end: just touching which

then swinging back to the waiting familiar
would be enough to establish the calm-browed
reasonableness of things. 'Nobody walks here.'
After the allotments, a railway line
then a hawthorn hedge hung with shreds of plastic.
Behind that again, some low changing sheds
and a football ground, also empty; churned mud.

I hesitated, then crossed the field. To souls
no definite place is granted. I was not told
I should find the river, but there it was
flowing, apparently, between low floodbanks
from a bend up there, where were some low trees
to disappear again under the motorway
that came into sight now, barring other progress.

Undeniably a river, with a river's purpose
and the purposes we find for rivers, as: to be the end
of a winter morning's walk, or to sit down
and weep by, or just chuck rubbish into:
about midstream were two cars
like dead crabs upside down exposing shafts
and exhausts. Their celebrated river was nothing, then:

not deep enough even to bury a wrecked car.

[30 October 1986]

FROM THE HEARTLAND

1

east
a mountain looking on Taupo
and ash sheeted plateaux sloping
tautly down to the Pacific

west
hidden by a near ridge
and the steel shed stark on the airstrip
a river runs through limestone to black sand

north
blue-shadowed Pirongia
beacons to watching shepherds
news of the fall of cities

south
is the cardinal of nostalgia:
all who are beloved by the gods
will see once more the snow on Taranaki

above   you
the warp and woof of jet trails
forever darning the huge hole in the sky—

        centre
yourself here, or anywhere
knee deep in the cocksfoot
of understocked paddocks

and feel a land holding itself together.

2

There are holes in the earth too:
narrow, secretive cracks
fringed by tangles of briar.

They will receive your stone
or any treasure
and wrap it in silence.

Some tip rubbish into them:
plastic bottles and fluids
may last longer than gold masks.

The bigger ones are caves
with rock lintels over choked entrances
but inside, huge as drowned cathedrals.

You showed me one
in a gesture of rare intimacy
something treasured from childhood

carefully equipping me with a torch
arranging stiff armour of old clothes
giving your hand to lead me under the earth.

[AS]

UNATTENDED CROSSING AHEAD

Some poems have no plan:
you simply have to be there to catch
the express when it whooshes through
and there's no timetable.

Oh they're not at all
like embroidery laid aside
taut in its drumlike frame
and awaiting a meditative hour.

Chance is all against them
they are unlikely as this love—
who knows when we'll meet again?
And it's not that we don't want to—

but then the children, the grave demands
of time and place, our health even—
the years compacting around our roots—
perhaps it'll always be like this?

Oh no, we say, we simply can't!
seeing it all so clearly:
and yet we're left breathless
standing here at the dusty crossing

while the red light bobs away
and the bell's clang chokes in a country silence
thinking, *I might have been on that train*
thinking, *it could have killed me.*

HARRIET MARTINEAU: FIRST INTIMATIONS
   OF POLITICS AND DEATH

The notion of death came to me early:
that was Nelson, and the black plumes waving
on the catafalque, and the black lines of print:

A NATION MOURNS ITS HERO. I had no idea
of the ponderousness of grief. From my mother's tears then
I learned of social being, and what follows from that.

Later I learned grief in its private dimension:
that would be when we were at Forth Lane
staying for weeks on one of those unexplained

holidays of childhood, and my aunt Martineau
died suddenly, in the night.
                          She had a sweet, pretty face
but her arms showed thin between glove and elbow

and she was, besides, peculiar in her manners.
My uncle loved her: before we reached the house
the sound of his grief came to us down the street

and I thought how thin are the walls of houses
and the worn cobbles under our feet. His wild
unpowdered hair was dreadful to us children

in that year of mourning. I also learned
that our earth swings free in space, and there is sky
all around us, and if we could tunnel

deep enough, we should see sky at the bottom
with stars moving across. Our small spades could dig
no further than shallow pits in which we lay

with folded hands, fancying we were dead.
Within a year my uncle married again
and was apparently happy. All this, before I was ten.

VARIATION ON AN OLD THEME

   for Catherine and Iain

For journeys into the past, you must
prepare quite carefully. Read
books on glaciation, on the geology

of the whole area. Bone up a little
on languages and customs. You knew them once
but you've forgotten. And don't
underestimate its capacity to surprise
or make a stranger of you.
                         Leaving
the roadside, clinking a lichened gate
pass into the shadow of a wood, dead pine
spongy underfoot, locate the stream
you remember as broadening here. Your way
is upward now. You climb
up a jumble of glacial till, the water
singing its way backwards in your head
to join the sea and its many islands
where your journey began.
                            Suddenly you come
upon a broad valley, quite secluded
a few sheep grazing among the mounds
of tumbled cottages, bees sailing
the waves of heather, and overhead
a buzzard circling in the cloudless sky.
You don't remember it
as being here, though it seems right
and the calm you feel quite natural. Unloop
the burden from your shoulders
and rest awhile. Maybe that ridge up there
brims back the lake you remembered, a wind
straight off the snow still crisping its waves
and a tarred boat upturned among the sedge
with no tracks leading to it, waiting for you.
But maybe not. This was a lake, too
though never in your time
or anyone's time. Stay here, float

gently in the sunlight filling this valley.
Let winter rage up there. Let
your young companion go in search of it.

COLLECTION DAY

I have not had the heart
to throw out these shoes, and so they lie
still mud-caked, at the bottom of a tin trunk.

Shoes should stand in neat pairs, or be walked in.
These lying in their bent shapes are like fragments
a boy breaks out from the context of a cliff

and stores in a box along with other stones
coins, cartridge cases, and other things labelled
with days and places, their native magic forgotten.

Death comes to all of us, watery eyed
trailing his black plastic bag and wanting things:
I've seen whole shopsfull of cracked shoes, in their pairs.

But today, woken early, just before dawn
by rain flung hard against the side of the house
I am not thinking of all that: today

we are going to take that famous walk
along the cliffs where the difficult path
lies deep in cowdung between the iron gates

past the cottage abandoned to the sea's encroachment
down the dene, and over the little bridge
then up again to the cliffs on the other side

where, if we are lucky, we shall just see
parting through the mist, the castle's twin towers
far to the north, and unattainable.

[14 February 1986]

PROPOSAL AT ALLANS BEACH

Basalt capes
thrust into the sea, the sea
curls back intimately
into the land, celebrating
a moody marriage. The wind here
saws into flesh like cord
but just around the sandhills
a small inland sea
dotted with maimais calmly sends
the sun back to heaven.
Even in winter you can lie
on its hard white beach
naked as if you'd just crawled
up from the sea like a fish with legs
and were looking around for a mate.
But up there above the ridges
it's always going on: the air
dividing, and pouring mist
down ngaio gullies, making sheep
get up and move, unveiling contours
taking them away again.
The whole place is a test site.
I've been bringing
people here for 20 years—
sometimes with a hard question

mostly to see how we match up
to its absolute background.
It never fails. Walk with someone
from the flax-hung cliff at one end
to the tidal creek at the other
and you'll know for sure
what's biting both of you
whether you could be friends for life
and lesser domestic truths. Of course
I had to be brought here once myself
on a particularly uninviting day.
Squinting up the dark green slopes
I knew I'd come home. Later
I sat by the lagoon a whole
sunfilled September day and planned
the work of a decade. And once
I came here with a friend and the rain
blew back into our faces and told us
we could never be the lovers
we thought we wanted to be.
I'm never alone here—
the place is full of ghosts.
With luck, you might see one
swimming naked in a rock pool
on the greyest day of the year.
It is a place for strong attachments:
friends, lovers, children.
I can't promise much
but you won't forget having been here
nor who you came with, and all
that followed, if it followed.

[9 August 1986]

MIND YOUR HEAD

Mind your head, you said, as I walked down the stair
Showing a sort of care, after the other sorts
That start with the play of hands, then go as far
As they ever can for us who are human and two—
And not the least sort either, you being one of those
Who feel any knock to others as to their own child
And that inside them still. And so I knew
All that it meant and was as grateful for that
As for any other single thing. I walked away
Still wearing the glowing shirt your arms had woven around
My shoulders and back all night

                              and yet I thought
Years later and somewhere else I'd heard you say
To someone else, not me, *O mind your head!*

The house being small and dangerous that way.

[14 June 1988]

HANGING THE WASHING OUT

I've set the programme: water trickles down like rain
in a mild depression: soon
the gradients will steepen, we'll have
a mini-hurricane which I'll call *felicity*
and imprison in a drum. The courtyard's piled
with snowdrifts of bedlinen, covers blue
as eggshell skies, layered flowerbeds
of pyjamas and shirts. Wind's tugging
at the slack halyard of clothesline, by lunch

there'll be a regatta in the garden. Birds
sing hallelujah, even the cat
regards me with respect. I'm the god around here,
I make things spin. Meanwhile there's time
for coffee and a letter, in the sun:
to you, or no-one.
                    If you missed anything
you'd miss this chore of sun and flapping shirts
bravely signalling another week gone by
in a measure of decency: you found it no small thing
to lie down each week between clean sheets,
to put off what's dirty and put on what's clean
and remember the camps of the world. You half foresaw
something like them, though now
you sleep or it's as if you slept. I'm still
writing, as though you might one day
wake up and read me, making the time of exile just
the eyeblink theologians say it is. I see this as part
of a professional life, of a vocation
made up of things you do in your spare time
and don't get paid for, hard
to justify to less fortunate friends. 'Why
does he have to *spend* his time like that?'
I read that as envy, knowing like Francesca
what felicity was like.
                        It never occurred to me
to resent anything you might have left me to do
by darting away one morning
with only the briefest of explanations
on some birdlike purpose of your own.
It might, I suppose. Unsemantic friends
enquire diplomatically after my anger—

just the one I don't feel, least of all today
surrounded by such cheerful mounds of washing.
But supposing you had asked—can I imagine
you rapping out some list of last instructions?

> *See to this and that. Write*
> *to her, to him.*
> *Make up your own mind*
> *about what you want to do with me.*
> *I don't want even to think about it.*
> *Don't grieve too much, but look after our son.*
> *Do all this, and do without me.*

Does it make things better or worse
to share such twilights, the slow
wedging of darkness into light? After words
the silence will anyway come, and the things
left unspoken and undone slowly multiply
until they are all that is. For our deathbed conversations
I have to look in books
or on the other side of the moon.

I'm doing it now, in this half public
monologue carefully starched and crimped,
into the best tone my words can supply
for wearing casually. 'Would he say that
if she were there?' Or: 'He shouldn't
let it all hang out so much.' Ah but
that's just my artfulness: hoping for an echo
as if there could be some particle of your voice
left clinging to a rock somewhere
or as if some expression of yours had passed
over the sea of faces, and had settled there,
a mote in the mind's eye.

I hope for it most
on such bright Saturdays as this.
From the first crawl
of daylight over my eyelids the first
sharp birdcall bringing its awareness
of today being special, first
of a new regime: what is this grey thing
that wakes with me before words or knowledge?
Later: how could I have forgotten? And later still
the doppelgänger who'll companion me
through all the day's demands, too close to challenge
yet never quite fitting in my private space.
                                                      Did you
ask me for this too? Neither
could have dreamed it, but how interesting
we'll find it to discuss
like a new idea or character in a novel
we were both reading. But then I think
there could never be an end to such discussion.
It would suck us up into its vortex
and whirl us round and round like leaves for ever.
Such things don't happen, they are literature
like this letter.
                I've lost
the mood in which I started it, but that
was in the programme too. What's spun
is spun. It's time
to go and hang the washing out.

[AS]

XI ∾ Being Outside Time: versions from Eugenio Montale (1985–87)

Only a few notes, a notebook which no editor
will ever publish, though it will perhaps be read
before some congress of demons and of gods
at an unknown date, being outside time.

—'My Friend Péa'

LETTER FROM THE RIVIERA DI LEVANTE

I should like these syllables
which I trace carefully for you
with a schoolboy's slow and painful hand
to reach you on some day of dark ennui
a day when the noon has no word for us
only the muttering of a gutter as it thaws
and we have not one reason left to oppose
to the minute as it sinks its tooth in us
and on every side the walls display their blankness
and the horror of living rises in our throat.

For surely you would remember me
your companion, and the hours we spent together
on those cobbled roads which cut their way
over our hills, stunted and clothed
in a lacework of bare branches—
no longer will you dream you run alone
under the wind-tossed vault of olive trees
stopping suddenly, then darting off
picked out, tiny, in the lightning's glare.
Oh slowly your memory will fill again
with the trees we knew then—
once more you will see
the barbed palm, the cedar
and your beloved medlar tree.

This is the memory of me I want
to implant in your life:
the faithful shadow, the companion who follows
and asks nothing for himself;
the image which issues from some moth-eaten print,

a lost memory of childhood, creating its moment of peace
in the day of torment;
and should at times some unknown power appear
to guide you through the entanglement
of hours that sear
oh beguile yourself that there's someone
who takes your hand for a moment
stealthily: and not
that angel of old sentimental books
but he: your quiet companion.

Listen still: I want to show you the thread
that so unites our being across the distance
that even if you were silent I would understand your meaning
as in your voice with its shadows, its transparence.
One day you told me of your childhood
passed among the dogs and the owls
of your hunting father: even then, I thought
you were permeated with that final
essence of phenomena in which the green
plants of life all have their root.
And so, while your playmates
passed their days in games or vain
concerns, unconscious, idle
already your few autumns
so clear of the world's stigma
grew aware of that enigma
which obsesses us: the Key.

While I too, growing up far
from the city, on the coast of the Levante
would climb nimbly before daybreak
up where the peaks were already whitening

surrounded by companions
their faces burned by the sun.
We'd whisper, clutching our ancient
muzzle-loaders in our hands
and panting as we pushed through the dark
then stopping to measure out
the black powder in our fingers
tamping the shot well down
to the end of our gun barrels.
Then I would wait, crouched in a bush
for the long line of wood pigeons
to ascend from the mists
and olive trees of the gullies
flying to the summit, now in shadow
now clear in the sun.
Slowly I drew bead on the grey leader
as he came on, and pressed
the trigger: the shot cracked in the blue
dry as splintering glass.
The struck bird staggered, left
a tuft of feathers hanging, and disappeared
turning like a scrap of paper in the air.
All around a mad flapping of wings
then the sudden renewal of silence.

I learned too in that growing time
seeing the hare killed in the vineyard
or the coppery squirrel bearing its tail
like a red torch from pine to pine
how such small companions of the *maquis*
might carry in their hides for years
small shot under the scars of old wounds

until some heavier piece of lead
brought them to the earth for ever.

If I seem to ramble it's only because
my memory of you has reawakened
this image of small wounded creatures;
it's because I can't think of our lives
disunited
without my heart awakening
those rudimentary feelings
and images which stand speechless before
the difficulty of our life today.
Yes, I have it—and you feel
it too: it's this, more than the shared sense
making us siblings of the trees and wind;
more than the cherished nostalgia of clear skies;
it's this that united us long ago—
our common awareness of being wounded
by some obscure spite in the universe.

And so to meet each other
was to find ourselves again
after the long years of exile
and in that instant time's reel
span us an unending thread:
unamazed, we walked on side by side
our words had no pretence, our faces wore no masks.
As I think now of certain moments in the past
when some nightfall, or renewal of light at dawn
would melt me with such feeling
that I searched in vain for someone to share
the hard burden of such wealth: yet all around
I felt the swirl of some benevolent power,

the unbidden entrance of a firm companionship;
and I know now that even in those moments
you were already at my side, that you are there still
though distant, in this wearisome day
that draws to an end, and will not see
the birth of any god;
and that we watch together, far in the distance, white
between the breakers and the mist
the spray-lashed cliffs of the Cinqueterre.

[November 1985, AS, MS-4150/004, variant MS-4150/006]

'SINCE LIFE ESCAPES US'

Since life escapes us
and he who tries to catch it back again
re-enters the labyrinth that gave us birth
where can we conceal them, if it's our aim
to survive with a few bare necessities
those objects which we always believed
were part of ourselves, and a part that was not to perish?
There existed once a small bookcase
which companioned Clizia on her travels, to hold
the writings of the Fathers, and poets of verbal wit.
Maybe it had
the virtue of being able to float
on the crest of the waves
once the deluge has drowned us all.
Surely some small bric-a-brac, yours if not mine
will outlast oblivion?

[MS-4150/003]

'GOOD LINUCCIA, YOU WHO CLIMB'

Good Linuccia, you who climb
life's road doubtfully
fearing time which cracks things,
the water which flows
under so many bridges
and is lost in the distance
I remember your pearl-grey Miramar
and the wood climbing up with its view
of the Arsenal and the smoke
losing itself in the morning mist, windy.
I remember your words, like your fan
exposed or closed with such swift grace
and your endless curiosity losing itself
in the Adriatic evening.
I remember …
              I remember nothing more. Such
time, such distance, such upright
walls. And then, such hell unleashed.

[MS-4150/003]

JOVIAN

On earth
millions of poems get written.
On Jupiter
it's quite different. Not one.
The Jovians have a science of their own
though no-one knows what it is.

One thing is certain:
mention the word 'man' up there
and they fall about laughing.

[AS, variant MS-4150/003]

MY FRIEND PÉA

When Leopoldo Fregoli heard death's tread
he donned his evening dress, set a flower in his buttonhole
and telephoned room service to send up lunch—
so Péa described to me the death of a man he greatly admired.
Another time, he told me of a winter at Sarzana
and all the ice of that long exile
with a stoic detachment to mask his pity—
pity for everything, for man, a little perhaps for himself.
I knew him for thirty years or more, as impresario,
as a sculptor of words, and a sculptor of men.
But today it seems that everyone's forgotten him
and the knowledge has somehow reached to where he is
and doesn't disturb him. He's taking notes
to tell us what it's like beyond the clouds
beyond the blue, beyond this rubbish tip of a world
in which by good grace we find ourselves thrown.
Only a few notes, a notebook which no editor
will ever publish, though it will perhaps be read
before some congress of demons and of gods
at an unknown date, being outside time.

[AS, variant MS-4150/003]

OBOE

Sometimes the Demiurge (God's fall-guy
stooge
and Viceregent of the here below)
ruminates upon the machinations
his enemies, God's faithful, attribute to him
because they haven't made the headlines, because
nobody knows they are eyes and ears.
But I am, at best, the oboe
which gives the keynote to the other instruments
and what follows may well be Pandemonium.
I have power, but I'm blind
though one day perhaps I too
will be able to see my master,
my enemy, but it occurs to me
that first someone will have to invent
a kind of picture of nothing, called Time
for my subjects to complain they're drowned in.

But, the Demiurge reflected, who knows when
my tyrant master will call upon me? He
hasn't made up his mind yet, and the oboe's out of tune.

[AS, MS-4150/003]

MONOLOGUE

It's long since I gazed
down from the parapet
looking for the arrival
of the horse-drawn omnibus
bringing the schoolchildren from the Barnabites.

Since whole stretches of time
appear to be cancelled
only a fool could believe
that life has no interruptions.
What I'm talking of here
isn't death then resurrection
but long descents to the Underworld, the turmoil
of something we hadn't quite reached
when the time came to break off.
But such would be the death we abhor
so let's be content with a turmoil
that sounds like a distant avalanche.
Listen: something's falling in the universe
something's looking for itself, for the sense
of beginning again
and we're dragged in its wake like jetsam.
Either that, or we fall each alone.

[AS, variant MS-4150/003]

'HOW THE HORIZON NARROWS'

How the horizon narrows
to that one fixed point.
Where have they gone, those huge aquariums
in which we used to drift suspended
without fear of line or hook?
Surely that was happiness:
to taste existlessness
yet to be alive, untouched by any fear
that this could never end.
A philosopher states (not all would agree)

that life here below is entirely improbable
with the corollary, I add, that it's also
out of joint. Most things that happen
tend to confirm it, only a few trivia
against. Such as the flight
of an ant entomologists have never studied
and perhaps never even heard of.

[AS, variant MS-4150/003]

HIDING PLACES

That reed bed where I used to go and hide
was sometimes lapped by the surf when it was high
but only spray ever entered that specimen
of before and after the Flood.
Larvae. Tadpoles. Insects. Empty cans.
And for one whole season, the visitation
of a hen with just one leg.
In the proper season the reeds would flaunt
their russet banners, and sometimes beyond the wall
you'd hear the solitary fluting of some bird
just as the poet said. But this one I imagined
as dark, ash-coloured, a blackbird
without its yellow beak but in recompense
awarded with that theme I heard years later
from the gentle lips of Manon in her flight.
But wasn't the fluting really from a lame hen
or some other bird, winged by a hunter?
Even then I never asked myself that question
though in the house there was a gun rack
with an old muzzle-loader, an obsolete weapon

that belonged once to some demented uncle.
Merely the sound of Manon's voice, just when you hear it
coming clearly out from that chorus of pimps
can carry me back, after so many years
to that reed bed by the sea, to that limping hen
and make me understand how the world has changed
for the worse of course even if it was absurd
to mourn for or even just remember
a foot that was lost to something that didn't
even know it and died among those reeds
while the water-blackbird was busy rehearsing a song
you can hear today in all the discotheques.

[AS, variant MS-4150/003]

A VISITOR

Whenever our aunt from Pietrasanta
appeared at the bottom of the avenue
we boys would run and hide in the attic.
It was her fault: she was old and a bore—
failings which even in those days
seemed incomprehensible, an insult, to the young.
My father would embrace her, listen attentively
to the torrent of misfortunes in which the poor old thing
swam like a fish, and then slip two sovereigns
into her purse, which was always open.
At last he would say:
you must hurry now, it'll soon be time
for the workers' train, that's your best one.
I haven't seen her since: today I suppose
she'd be a hundred at least. Yet when I read or hear

the name PIETRASANTA, I think of those few sovereigns,
of the misery of the world and its mischances—
such as having a grandparent, or being the great-grandchild
of god knows who, who never even lived.

[AS, variant MS-4150/003]

SUCCULENTS

A distant relative of mine was a collector
of succulents. People came from all over
to see them. Even de Lollis came
that celebrated (!) dabbler in prose poems.
They used to foregather at the 'Monterosa'
(a restaurant for bachelors, long gone).
Today the greenhouses, the plants, the visitors
are no longer there: not even the garden
where all these marvels were to be seen.
As for my relative—
it's as if he never existed. He'd been a student
at Zurich, and managed to fail every subject
but when our country started to change for the worse
he would shake his head and say, well now, at Zurich ...

I don't know what meaning the ridiculous has
in the Being/Nothingness in which we live:
there's bound to be one, perhaps not the worst.

[AS, variant MS-4150/003]

WITHIN/WITHOUT

When reality becomes disjointed
(if it was ever one) and some part of it
forms over us like a crust
then a whiff of ether (not the surgical kind)
informs us that memory's just a piece of eternity
wandering around at a loss
and waiting to find itself again in us.
It's why I see you now
turning back from the gangway
of the liner taking you to New England
or: us together, on the verandah
of the 'Annalena', busy
hunting for fleas through
the rhymes of the venerable
but itchy John Donne
and we've laid aside Meister Eckhart
and all such visionary abysses.
But now the phone rings and a voice
I hardly recognise says ciao
then adds I must tell you this, after thirty years:
my name is Giovanna, I was Clizia's friend
and I sailed on that liner with her. Not a word more,
not even see you again, that would be ridiculous
for both of us.

[AS, variant MS-4150/003]

'MY SWISS WATCH WAS FAULTY'

My Swiss watch was faulty
it had a habit of stealing from time:
hence it was only 5, not 6
when I sat down at the Caffè San Marco.
It seemed a small thing, a piece of luck even
this distancing oneself from an appointment
though upon her the time weighed heavily
and her pallor, in time, became my own.
How long should our final (if
that is what they are) goodbyes last? There's no
Manual of Love which properly explains
the disappearance of a god. In such cases
it hardly seems to matter
whether a watch goes slow or fast.

[AS, variant MS-4150/003]

'TO ME IT'S JUST IMPOSSIBLE'

To me it's just impossible
my divine one, my all
that what remains of you is less
than the greenish-red spark
of a firefly that's outlived the season.
The truth is, not even the whole
body of the incorporeal could outweigh
the heaven you fill.
It's only when the letters
of the cosmos get jumbled
into nonsense that they say
anything sensible about you.

[AS, MS-4150/003]

'WIPE YOUR GLASSES IF THEY ARE DIMMED'

Wipe your glasses if they are dimmed
by any mist or vapour in the Beyond
and look around and down: can you see
any sign of what your apprentice years
called life? For us too,
the living or so-called it's hard
to believe that we're just imprisoned here
and waiting for the lock to be sprung
upon some more terrifying happiness.

It's noon, someone with a napkin is coming
to tell us to hurry because dinner is served—
dinner or refreshments or something of the kind—
but the train doesn't slacken in its headlong course.

[AS, variant MS-4150/003]

A PUPIL OF THE MUSES

Pack your suitcase, my child
with all your poems sacred and profane
pack it
and throw it into the river.
The river will carry it far away and leave it
wedged among the boulders and half buried.
Maybe someone will rescue
a leaf or two, perhaps the worst:
what does it matter? The taste
of the Gods is different from ours
and whoever said it was better?
What matters is that from

the whole boiling something confronts us and says
you don't know me, I don't know you—still,
we share the lot, the god-given madness
of being here and not there, alive
or so we call ourselves, my child.
Leave now. And don't
keep your luggage locked too tight.

[AS, variant MS-2674/190, MS-4150/003]

DAYBREAK

The writer imagines   not
to speak of the poet
that when he's dead his works
will render him immortal.
The hypothesis isn't new:
I give it you for what it's worth.
But in the case of the warbler
who's eating his breakfast on the lawn below
I imagine nothing of the sort:
he's sure of life.
               The philosopher
who lives on the ground floor
has more than one doubt
and as for the world—
it can do without everything, even itself.

[AS, variant MS-2674/190, MS-3619/026, MS-4150/003]

THE COASTGUARD'S HOUSE

You don't remember the coastguard's house
on its overhanging cliff above the reef:
desolate, it awaits you since that evening
the swarm of your thoughts entered it
and stayed there, without finding peace.

For years the southerly's lashed its ancient walls
and the sound of your laughter is no longer gay:
the dice box rattles madly but the dice
don't fall out for us as they did once.
You don't remember: another time stands in the way
of memory: a thread's wound up again.

I hold one end of it still, but the house
is growing distant and the weathervane
smoke-blackened on its roof veers pitiless.
I hold one end of the thread, but you remain
elsewhere, not breathing in the darkness here.

Oh the horizon ever in flight, where the blaze
of a petrol tanker's light is rarely seen.
Is this where we cross over? (and still

the surf breaks at the foot of the crumbling cliff ...)
You don't remember the house of my evening here
and I no longer know who goes, and who stays
on its overhanging cliff above the reef.

[2 April 1987, MS-4150/003]

Sources

PUBLICATIONS

(a) Poetry

Recreations (Wai-te-ata Press, 1967, 1970)
Letters from Ephesus (Bibliography Room, University of Otago, 1970)
Courting Death (Wai-te-ata Press, 1984) [CD]
The Entrance to Purgatory (John McIndoe, 1986) [TETP]
Winter Walk at Morning, posthumous, ed. Bill Manhire and Don McKenzie (Victoria University Press, 1991) [WWAM]

(b) Non-fiction

'De natura pueri, ch. 13' in *Corpus Hippocraticum*, ed. Robert Joly (University of Mons, 1977)

HOCKEN COLLECTIONS HOLDINGS

(a) Lonie, Iain: Papers (ARC-0671), principally:

MS-2674/104
MS-2674/105 (c. 1948–53)
MS-2674/106
MS-2674/108
MS-2674/110
MS-2674/111 (personal correspondence, 1966–70)
MS-2674/112 (personal correspondence, 1952–56)
MS-2674/143 (c. 1964–68)
MS-2674/184 (c. 1983, TETP)
MS-2674/185 (c. 1983–84, TETP)
MS-2674/186 (c. 1980s, TETP)

MS-2674/187 (TETP)
MS-2674/188 (1985, TETP)
MS-2674/189 (1985, TETP)
MS-2674/190 (Montale)
MS-2674/192 (1981–84)
MS-2674/249
MS-3619/005
MS-3619/007
MS-3619/009 (CD)
MS-3619/012 (1983, CD)
MS-3619/017 (1984, CD)
MS-3619/020
MS-3619/021 (c. 1977)

MS-3619/022 (1986, TETP)
MS-3619/027
MS-3619/028 (1949–51)
MS-3619/029 (1952–53)
MS-3619/030 (1950–51)
MS-3619/031 (1953)
MS-3619/032
MS-3619/033 (1954)
MS-3619/034
MS-3619/035 (1956–58)
MS-3619/036 (1955)
MS-3619/037
MS-3619/038 (1969–71)
MS-3619/041 (1971)
MS-3619/042 (September 1975
to March 1983)
MS-3619/043 (1986–87)
MS-3619/044
MS-3619/081 (family photographs)
MS-3619/190 (1986, Montale)
MS-4150/001 ('Bricolage')
MS-4150/002 (letters from Ann Somerville, 1988)
MS-4150/003 (Montale)
MS-4150/004
MS-4150/005 (WWAM)
MS-4150/006 (1988, WWAM)
MS-4150/007 (1987, WWAM)
MS-4150/008

(b) Brasch, Charles: Literary and personal papers

Correspondence with Iain Lonie [63691 MS-0996-002/221]
'Seen but not dealt with' Letters, surnames G–L [69497 MS-0996-003/215]

(c) Reeves, Trevor: Papers

'Readings and Discussions on the Muse' [264965 MS-3737/164]

ANN SOMERVILLE PAPERS [AS]

Private collection. Manuscript and typescript poems accompanying letters from Iain Lonie to Ann Somerville, dating from 1985–88.

PERIODICALS

Landfall Volume 6 Number 3 September 1952
Landfall Volume 13 Number 1 March 1959
Landfall Volume 19 Number 2 June 1965
Landfall Volume 21 Number 2 June 1967
Otago University Review 1952
Otago University Review 1888–1971

Notes

Whatever importance posterity had for Iain Lonie as a poet, at his death he was known as a medical historian. Within six months his research papers went to the Wellcome Library of Otago Medical School, whereas his literary and personal papers did not reach the safe haven of the Hocken Collections for another two decades.

While editing I have made thousands of decisions about which poems and which versions of which poems to adopt; to document them all would be to bury the verve of living verse in a volume the size of a funeral monument. For those who wish to dig I have given the source(s) of each text that has not been previously collected. The volumes seen through the press by the poet are reproduced verbatim, with dates of composition appended when known – although the poet rarely dated his texts and a handwritten retrospective calendar in MS-2674/187 is treated as suspect in the absence of other verification.

Don McKenzie (see the biographical note to 'Letter from a Ferry'), who oversaw Lonie's posthumous *Winter Walk at Morning*, said, 'In some ways I think Iain might have preferred the cleanliness of silent editorial decisions (even if the odd one was wrong). For the most part the reader is having to take my decisions on trust in any case' [Letter to Fergus Barrowman, 17 January 1991, MS-4150/006]. Those poems from which the collection was compiled have been checked against extant manuscript and typescript versions; late handwritten additions which Lonie made to otherwise clean typescripts have been incorporated from the Ann Somerville papers.

One caveat: Lonie habitually copied out texts he admired without identifying the source. Standard methods of identifying and dating are of no help when the origin of the content is in question. An editor necessarily operates, in good faith, on partial knowledge. Ours is not a perfect world; errors of judgement can occur, neighbouring stock may be herded into the barn, and apologies could be in order. I have done my best.

I ∽ Digging to the Antipodes

While still a student Iain Lonie drafted this preface, which is earnest and ingenuous, to his juvenilia:

> The following poems were all written in my seventeenth year, within a period of about five months.
>
> I believe I am as much aware of their faults as anyone. They all abound in technical errors. They are odd, or obscure, or flat. All betray a great lack of experience in the medium of language. Influenced predominantly by modern poetry, they attempt to use as their framework what is catchy and superficial in that. All this is due to the fact that they are the verses of an adolescent; and as such I publish them.
>
> It is difficult to judge one's own writing dispassionately, even after a long lapse of time, for one always unconsciously fills up the gaps with the personal, uncommunicated experience. Nevertheless, I think that each one of these poems has its good points; and I hope that I shall not be accused of undue egotism when I claim that, as a whole, these poems are better than the average of adolescent poetry. For one thing, the adolescent in this case took both himself and his poetry extremely seriously. He was interested in nothing but poetry, and read and wrote nothing but poetry. Nothing could shake his firm belief that he would one day become the star of the poetic world. And this overwheening confidence was of value to him in that it supplied him with energy for his intense pursuit of poetry.
>
> For the sake of that adolescent, who was, despite all his faults, genuinely interested in communication for itself, I have collected these poems of an adolescent; and I hope that they will somewhere find an audience. [MS-2674/105]

On 25 August 1948 Lonie made his first submission to *Landfall*. Charles Brasch returned the work. Then, on 14 September 1948, Lonie responded:

> I am enclosing these three poems. Although they are not good enough for publication, your criticism would be a very great help.

> I am sixteen, and I have been writing for a year. I can't write nearly as well as I would like to write, but my poems seem to be improving gradually.
> Do you think that I should continue? [63691 MS-0996-002/221]

The early poems show sun damage from overexposure to the brilliant Auden. On 22 August 1951 Lonie commented: 'Read somewhere: a remark of Spender's on Auden that he was only a "brilliant commentator". Are any of us anything more? I don't think I want my songs to be anything but authentic comments on the life of a mythical man of action' [MS-3619/028]. But on 16 November 1951 he admitted:

> I told Colin Newbury [editor of the *Otago University Review*, future Oxford historian] this morning that I was thinking of giving up poetry for something worthwhile—in my case, at least, poetry is fundamentally dishonest. He said that having found poetry was too hard, I was looking for something more 'noble', hoping it might be easier. Damn Liar. It's true, none the less. But so is my side of the story. Poetry seems to be my revenge on society for always being awkward, talking in the wrong accent at schools, being bullied, plain, unpopular. Or is it? If it is only that, I shall never write, for if the artistic impulse is such a bastard child as to be engendered by maladjustment, 'I'll none of it.' [MS-3619/028]

A maturing Lonie, then at King's College, Cambridge, told Brasch on 12 January 1956:

> I haven't read much lately, outside Classics—although I bought *The Shield of Achilles* as soon as I saw it in Heffers. But however resplendent its yellow cover, and however great the thrill of seeing a new Auden, at the end one is woefully disappointed—or so I was. I never did read poetry intellectually—could never give a paraphrase of a 'difficult' poem—but Auden always used to, in certain lines and passages, excite me intensely and present me with a sort of new tool for quarrying into reality. Of course all *I* produced was pastiche, but I did feel that I could have learnt more from Auden than from any other contemporary poet. But there was nothing of this in his new book—flat ginger beer, astringent but somehow heavy. [63691 MS-0996-002/221]

'RUBBING MY HAND ALONG THE ROUGH-CAST WALL'

Lonie regarded this as his earliest *steady* step towards Mount Parnassus:

> This is probably the first coherent poem that I ever wrote. I had been reading Eliot most, and was fascinated by the imagery of his earlier poems. Auden I had just heard of. The main idea was a small pebble that I imagined 'foam-white' with 'delicate blue veins'. Secondary to this was the idea that squared blocks of stone, from a palace, might in time be taken by the sea, broken into fragments which would be smoothed. Thus a man in the twentieth century might pick up a pebble which had formed part of a palace thousands of years before. Then there was the third idea of the general ugliness of 'suburban villas' and all they implied. The fourth idea was the somewhat hackneyed one of the impermanence of man's works:
>
> > 'But spit, and smile …'
>
> (although the last line of the poem refers to the 'pebble on beach' above).
>
> These were the ideas as they occurred to me. But, if the poem is not altogether too obscure, the fourth idea seems to have the most importance. I didn't do justice to the second.
>
> There is a certain control of line in the poem, and a feeling for exotic imagery. There is not much that is superfluous, for I had gained some mastery (apparently) over my emotions. But the poem is obviously written in early youth, and is inconsequential in its effect. [MS-3619/027]

'NOW SPRING DAWNS IN OUR MONTHS OF PASSION'

On the page immediately after the third (and last) draft of this, Lonie complains:

> I was going to write a poem this evening, but I got hold of the wrong kind of thought, and wrecked everything. Anyhow, I think it was one of those moods where one feels one must do something of the sort, to pep up one's ego. And if one (how I hate that 'one') is fool enough to start, all that comes forth is a formal diarrhoea of metre and stock conceit. That comes forth in my case, anyway. I am one of those unfortunate people who have an entire inability to appreciate poetry—and yet I want to write the stuff. Odd! [MS-3619/034]

FRAGMENT

Shortly after drafting this fragment Lonie attempted to ring-fence his ambition: 'I must be strong with myself, and forget publication and all its attendant glories. If I can reach a state when I genuinely don't care, I may get something done. (Or does it have any effect other than foolish eagerness and premature deliveries? Yet it may have a genuine effect on what I write, always)' [MS-3619/027]. But in 1952, peevishly optimistic, he had observed:

> It's all very well to start off by reading and discussing your poems among friends—it's a good stimulus, one needs it—but to have no other prospect—never to reach a larger public because it isn't there—to have books published at the Caxton Press only to look well on your own bookshelf, and on the bookshelves of those who, probably, have read all the poems before—that damns anyone's attempts at writing well. I want—must have, if I'm to achieve anything—a huge audience and the highest standards of criticism in the world. With the best of intentions, it is impossible in New Zealand.
>
> I may as well publish poems all my life in a University newspaper. It's so fatally, inevitably easy in this intellectual hothouse to produce slipshod verse. [MS-3619/029]

SONG

The image of the gunmen is borrowed from Cecil Day-Lewis.

SCOTTISH MILL TOWNS

A few pages after drafting this poem a querulous yet defensive Lonie tells himself off:

> To say 'you have written verse which for your age is quite intelligent, and it is likely that you will become some sort of poet' is not enough. I write verse, and have a strong desire to write poetry, yet that does not imply that I have poethood in me. Just at present I believe I have not. I think it is very likely that a person who has not poetic sensibility in him may start writing verse (and very many youths who are not poets do so), which habit may continue until he becomes

fairly proficient in the art of imitation. But a poem, which is always highly original, is not an imitation.

Perhaps it is ridiculous to rely on poets' accounts of their youthful experience in the matter of writing poetry. Yet every one seems to have had some sudden revelation, which coloured his whole life forthwith. But I 'rather liked' the idea of writing verse, as I 'rather liked' the idea of taking up fencing, etc., only the verse habit lasted longer than the fencing. Now my verse seems at first appearance to demonstrate a definite talent for poetry, and an understanding of contemporary poetry particularly. Yet I don't think this is true. I fail to detect in it the tiniest seed of latent originality (i.e. poethood). I think that my habit is merely a cloak, or rather a protective suit of armour, the bright and powerful appearance of which is a sad contrast to the emaciated and weak stripling inside. [MS-3619/027]

'GIVE TO ALL YOUTH THIS I HAVE KNOWN'

Alongside the poem, which must be earlier than its appearance in the source notebook, Lonie comments: 'The poem opposite was written when I was dominated by Auden. This is apparent from language and idea. The impulse is sustained throughout fairly well—no flagging off towards the end, which is only too common among my other poems' [MS-3619/027].

On 10 July 1971, now the author of two slim volumes, Lonie watched his early idol topple:

> In the evening, Queen Elizabeth Hall, poetry reading, Auden, shambling toward microphone, mustard coloured suit & pink shirt, read three long, boring, & trivial poems, 'Talking to dogs', 'Talking to mice', 'Talking to myself', in an almost totally indistinct voice (as if mouth filled with treacle, & no teeth besides), microphone broke down at one stage, too far away to see his face, after which he retired to back of stage & donned a pair of dark glasses & looked bored for rest of performance. Oh the god of one's youth—blurred in sight, inaudible in sound, faded. [MS-3619/041]

'AT WHORING I WAS INEFFECTUAL'

Two isolated lines in black ink below and to the left of an unrelated draft in blue ink.

In a later notebook there is an entry, dated 5 May 1951, that is an indirect gloss upon this squib: 'At the moment the problems are marriage and sex, frustration of ambition, and "making the best of things". None are insoluble, but I have no inner strength, except occasionally the deceptiveness of self-conceit' [MS-3619/030].

By 15 May 1952 Lonie was short with those who assumed intellectual superiority over the majority: ' "A cell of good living in a corrupt society" is what Baxter said the poet must be. This is nonsense. The poet must learn that he is corrupt as any of them, and not live in a cell at all' [MS-3619/029].

WICKLIFFE BAY: *Morning Calm*

In a separate notebook there is an entry, headed 'Marlborough Sounds '50', that clarifies Lonie's uncertain relations with the external—human and inhuman—world:

> This is my feeling of hell. A feeling in this place of detachment from all familiar surroundings: a feeling of imprisonment too; and sometimes inimical nature: frowning hills and cold water. A superficial companionship among the damned. But in moments of pain—and Hell is a place of pain—no real communication is possible. With me: pain, and a panic stricken desire to escape.

A later entry, probably from early May 1951, further defines Hell:

> Hell—a perpetual contemplation of our own deficiency—I heard this definition somewhere. And for a moment this evening I despaired as I thought of the ultimate human selfishness. There is no kindness, no charity: what we give we give only because we know we shall receive ten times only. Affection and love are a kind of spiritual bargaining.
>
> If we are ultimately selfish, we are ultimately quite alone, each one of us. A proposition that is glib enough on paper, and holds hell in its realisation. [MS-3619/030]

On Tuesday, 20 February 1951, the 19-year-old had speculated:

If I were to commit suicide now, they would say of me—'neurotic with suicidal tendencies' and wag their heads over my record. They would know nothing of the terrible fear of insanity, knowing nothing of the utter loneliness of soul that insanity means. But I have seen it, I have lived with the damned, and I fear it, and sometimes anticipate it. Tonight I have very little hope. [MS-3619/028]

LETTER FROM A FERRY

The dedicatee is Donald Francis McKenzie (1931–1999). A lifelong friend, his early letters to Lonie are collected in MS-2674/112, including this tribute from 27 March 1953:

> I think you realise the debt I owe to you—no, not perhaps a debt, for it can never be repaid, but that capacity of yours to bring me glimpses of another world, one full of subtle nuances and bold striking beauties, and beyond that again, glimpses of eternity and all that it means. Your conversation, your letters, you, have been *my* awakening into consciousness and understanding in a very real way.

In 1962 McKenzie founded the Wai-te-Ata Press, which published both *Recreations* (1967, 1970) and *Courting Death* (1984). The founding director of Downstage, New Zealand's first professional theatre company, he was Professor of English Language and Literature at Victoria University (1969–87), then Professor of Bibliography and Textual Criticism at Oxford University (1989–96).

On 3 November 1988, writing to the poet's eldest daughter Bridie after her father's suicide, McKenzie reflected:

> My own reactions over the months since June have continued to show the same pattern [to that of another old friend Peggy Garland], an alternation of brief moments of uncontrolled grief with calm acceptance—this last, I hope, out of respect for Iain's resolution of the lifelong tension he'd felt between his acutely sensitive response to the sensuous pleasures of the world and the purity of intellect that led him into a fascination with the absoluteness of death. The two did receive, I believe, a remarkably consistent synthesis in his poetry where what was sensuous in his nature, and in language itself, shines through with a sight-cleansing lucidity. I continue to think that in

his last moments he saw with absolute clarity what he was doing. Like his poetry, and his conversation when it pursued a point with his exciting mix of rigour and finesse, it required the exclusion of everything subordinate to his immediate concern. [MS-3619/005]

Perhaps Lonie typically had temporal clarity but, in consequence, an uncommon need for the true absolute of death? On 3 February 1955 the young man confided to his diary: 'Glad to find myself still mildly unbalanced—I may topple into truth one day' [MS-3619/035].

from REMARKS ON A LANDSCAPE PAINTING

The lines reproduced here are the third and final part of the poem.

WITCH

This animist association of women, witchcraft and wood is reworked more memorably in the final section of 'Crusoe's Canoe':

> I see something of the art, it has more
> of woman's witchcraft than it has of detail
> a thinking yourself into things. The art
> is to take trees apart in so gentle a way
> that they'll hold themselves together for you
> in a different shape, the living vessel ... [TETP]

THE ACHAEANS

On 15 January 1958 Lonie wrote to the patrician Brasch:

> At the moment I'm reading American verse, some of which I find particularly exciting and helpful. Robert Lowell and Richard Wilbur I find, in their highly different ways, very interesting, although I only know them in anthologies. But the ones I shall go back to again and again are Wallace Stevens and Marianne Moore ... Also Chinese poetry. But I find I can learn nothing from translations—or, indeed,

poetry in another language. It is rhythms that stimulate me. Oddly, Rilke is an exception here.

On 5 May 1958 Lonie submitted these two sonnets, with other poems, to *Landfall*. In his covering letter he advised: '"The Achaeans" only ran to five sonnets altogether and I don't think the others were much good.'

On 1 August 1958 an acute Charles Brasch responded: 'I like both sonnets (but to what exactly does their in 1.9 of the second refer? not surely only to the sentries of 1.2?). A pity you don't think much of the others of the sequence, because these seem to need support from other pieces, good though they are.'

On 29 September 1958, accepting some poems for *Landfall* (March 1959), the older poet continued: 'The two sonnets of "The Achaeans" should go together (by the way, I don't much like "Dim permanences under the Protean tide"; and shouldn't it be protean as an ordinary adjective?)' [63691 MS-0996-002/221]. The first sonnet, 'Their forefathers, moving through a fluent', was subsequently revised and collected as section 16 of *Recreations* (see p. 110).

ELEGY, ARMIDALE CEMETERY

It was originally called 'The Tree and the Shell'. On 16 October 1958 Lonie informed Brasch, with whom he was now in friendly if not disinterested correspondence: 'As a matter of fact, all the poems I wrote between August of last year and February of this got lost, and I had to reconstruct one from memory—the others are in limbo. It's a pity, but no doubt the fittest survived' [63691 MS-0996-002/221].

DIALOGUE

In the same notebook, dated 15 June 1958, is a more utilitarian companion piece under the heading 'Rules':

1 Put a piece of work away while you're still interested in it.
2 Nothing was ever achieved by concentrating one's activities prematurely.

3   Your first duty is grace to those with whom you are in immediate contact—your children & wife.
4   Succeed—and don't lose your capacity for imagining other possibilities.
5   An ambitious man cannot dispense with clean collars.
6   Nothing matters very much, except that you should not be selfish. Take risks by all means—a risk means jumping from a secure and comfortable position into the unknown. It doesn't mean running away.
7   Everyone has enough time to waste it.
8   Never concentrate on one thing exclusively.
9   All the rules are contained in one: don't get exhausted. [MS-3619/037]

from THE WIND AT RIMINI

Section 17, 'Death', of Lonie's collection *Recreations* (1967) was originally the sixth and closing section of this earlier sequence, which in June 1965 appeared complete in *Landfall*.

A manuscript in MS-2674/143 assigns the unlikely title 'Lawnmower' to a sequence comprising 'Her Room', 'Her Dreams', 'The Wind at Rimini', 'Last Night', 'I drove past …', and 'Death'. Section 3, '*Così vidi venir, traendo guai, / ombre portate dalla detta briga*' ('So did the shades I saw approaching, borne / by that assailing wind, lament and moan', trans. Allen Mandelbaum), is from Dante's *Inferno*, v:48–49.

ELEGY TO MAECENAS

As Wordsworth affirmed, *There was a boy …* This is where the young Lonie learned how to whistle in a distinctive way. With 'Ugolino and His Sons' and the unbuttoned 'Short Story', it is his most memorable work from the 1960s, yet all three were set aside rather than collected. There are two classical precursors. 'Elegiae in Maecenatem' dates from 8 BCE; it was traditionally assigned to Virgil, but that is impossible; one alternative is Albiovanus Pedio. The opening of Propertius' *Elegies*, Book II (c. 24 BCE) honours Maecenas (68–8 BCE), who was an advisor to the Emperor Augustus and the patron of Horace and Virgil.

II ～ Recreations (1967, 1970)

On 4 October 1967 publisher Don McKenzie reported for Wai-te-ata Press:

> At long last I can send you a copy of *Recreations* in something like its final form … It's been a long job, and I'm sorry that I haven't been more efficient over it, but given our slender resources in money, materials and (as it happened) labour, I'm not wholly displeased with the results. It has been running parallel with another booklet too—Alistair Campbell's *Blue Rain*, which is now virtually completed. You have been remarkably patient. [MS-2674/104]

Section 1 ('Shop windows turn their light upon the street') was written for Lonie's second wife, Judith Black, whom he met in Sydney. In June 1968 Alan Roddick, reviewing the collection for *Landfall*, noted that 2 ('It may happen at any time') and 10 ('One may grow angry with it') were 'originally published in *Landfall* (March 1958) as parts of a sequence entitled "Poems of Sickness"'. The middle section of that earlier sequence was 19 ('The worst part is the waking dream'). In addition, an earlier version of section 16 (Their forefathers, moving through a fluent') was part of 'The Achaeans' (see pp. 76–77), while 17 ('Death') was once the final section of 'The Wind at Rimini'. Section 15 was originally part of a sequence entitled 'Electra in Sydenham' [MS-2674/143]. After reading *Recreations* Lonie's eldest son Jonathan wrote:

> I hope you keep writing happily and contentedly perhaps you need more encouragement … well I read your book again one sunny Sunday when I was alone: it was extremely beautiful poetry especially part III, I had never realised how close to Donovan it is, I suppose I judge all poetry by his, but it is perfect poetry and very musical, it is like the sea touching the sand at Karitane or like the fisher boats drifting past the caves in the evening time. I can well imagine you at my age intending to become one of the best poets in the world but it doesn't matter at all if you don't get to be well known it won't be the fault of the poetry. [c. 1968, MS-2674/106]

III ∾ Living for Others

'THE SNOW MELTS QUICKLY FROM THE HILLS'

Lonie perceptively wrote below the poem: 'Lacks the necessary glue of Art.' By 1954 he had determined that 'The ability of a poet to be a poet certainly depends largely upon his ability to organise apparently conflicting experience, to be aware of connections between diverse things whose connections are not apparent to ordinary people' [MS-3519/033].

'IF IN THE MORNING'

Marked by Lonie: 'Poem I can't publish—but here it is' [MS-2674/104].

ERINNA'S LAMENT FOR BAUKIS

After 'The Distaff' by Erinna (fourth century BCE). Italian archaeologists excavating Oxyrhynchus discovered papyrus which contained the 54-line fragment that is the basis for this free version. A typescript of this 'riff' was presented to a poetry discussion group hosted by Charles Brasch on 1 August 1968.

UGOLINO AND HIS SONS

Submitted by invitation with 'The Wind at Rimini', 'Four Sydney Photographs', 'Letter from Ephesus' and 'Street' to Charles Monteith (then a director and subsequently the chairman of Faber and Faber) on 2 January 1968, when Lonie affirms 'they are all recent'—even though parts of 'The Wind at Rimini' were drafted in the late 1950s. 'Ugolino' was subsequently rejected by Monteith, as it was by Robin Dudding of *Landfall* in a letter dated 4 October 1968. This text incorporates handwritten changes apparently made after that *Landfall* rejection.

The epigraph 'Padre mio, ché non mi aiuti' ('Father, why do you not help me?', trans. Allen Mandelbaum), from Dante's *Inferno* XXXIII:69, echoes Christ's words on the cross as recounted in Matthew 27:46.

IV ∾ Letters from Ephesus (1970)

> There are some things
> Which should never be seen—
> Such as bone. ['Street Scene']

The figure of the voyeur, an onlooker who reports but without the power to change, informs this brief suite of poems. On 20 February 1969 Lonie speculated more directly than he does in most poems (except for 'Studies 4: Ibycus'):

> Suppose that we were naked, caught *de improviso* and suddenly exposed to the stare of some stranger, who leers and shuffles in embarrassment, not sure whether to make a joke or an approach of some kind. He is insignificant. What would matter is that she would be new, be suddenly made conscious of being naked. For a moment she becomes real again, utterly desirable (only these moments recur repeatedly). It is her shame, her self-consciousness, that makes her desirable. Or so Sartre would say. [MS-3619/038]

V ∾ Seeing the Island

While Lonie felt constrained by the smallness (and the small-mindedness) of New Zealand, Europe brought a different sort of claustrophobia: 'Too many things, too many people. One's self-esteem, if one has the wrong sort to begin with, is utterly crushed underneath it: the world's composed of things and of persons, and each one is, alas, unique' [14 February 1971, Florence, MS-3619/038].

AFTERNOON TEA IN THE EAST

The occasion of this poem was Lonie's first visit to East Germany. On 10 March 1971, he reports:

> To Herr Haarig's and Frau Kollesch's flat. Very luxurious—antique furniture, many rooms, splendid tiled stove, very warm. But Haarig's father was a member of the party in the 1930s, and Haarig himself fled with his father to Russia, where he was educated. Probably it is for this reason that they have as many and as different kinds of books as one could possibly want. Haarig himself an enormously attractive character—large head, small neat clean hands, with a large ring, very eloquent and cheerful, highly intelligent, extroverted, possibly capable of evil—altogether like a character from Dostoievsky. A complete contrast to the sad ironic Stropmeier. We talked, in German, of academic conditions, of the possibility of my doing a text of Galen, etc. Very good tea, in Meissen cups. [MS-3619/038]

ODE TO WALTER

Walter Ulbricht (1893–1973), first secretary of the Socialist Unity Party (1950–71) and head of state (1960–73) in the German Democratic Republic (East Germany).

WEST BERLIN: UNORCHESTRATED NOTES

On 22 February 1971 Lonie sent an untitled variant version of this to Charles Brasch from Berlin [MS-0996-003/215].

MEMORIES OF ITHACA

On 13 July 1971 Lonie and his wife Judith were there: 'Ithaca. The strong wind moaning eerily through blue shutters in our bedroom, an eternal sound' [MS-3619/041].

CHANGE OF SEASON ON THE WAY TO THE STATION

This alludes to Janet Frame, whose first collection of stories was *The Reservoir*, and whose first (and, in her lifetime, only) collection of poetry was *The Pocket Mirror*: 'the reservoir's surface a pocket mirror'.

TERRITORIAL DISPUTE

Originally entitled 'Love Poem'; Lonie never cancelled this, instead appending the title used here with a question mark in front of it [MS-2674/110].

PIONEERS

The draft appears in MS-3619/042 between entries dated 6 and 13 January 1976. On New Year's Day Lonie was reading *The Last of England* by Peter Porter, a significant influence on his late poems with their stately conversational wit.

'I AM A SMALL BOY'

On 18 January 1976, in the notebook entry immediately before this, the peripatetic and rueful poet writes: 'Sunday night with the Thorntons—so profoundly established. That is the kind of life that I am envying now, when we are throwing so much of our existence away instead of quietly gathering it around ourselves' [MS-3619/042].

'A BEAUTIFUL DARK HAIRED GIRL RUNS'

A notebook entry; it is not obvious that Lonie regarded this as a poem but his deliberate contrast of the two parts, together with the felicitous lineation, makes it one.

FRIENDS AT THE FUNERAL

In an entry from his diary (December 1982 to March 1983) Lonie echoes this poem: 'Everyone gets it wrong—nobody can share this place with me' [MS-3619/042].

HOMOEOTELEUTON

A rhetorical figure consisting of the use of a series of words with the same or similar endings, or an error in copying caused by the occurrence of similar endings in two neighbouring words or lines.

VI ∾ Courting Death (1984)

The Muse and ghost of these poems is Judith (Black) Lonie, the poet's second wife. She died without warning, of an aortic aneurism, on 18 December 1982. Seven weeks after, as letters of condolence continued to arrive, Iain Lonie wrote:

> I must follow her. The trouble is, although we have countless metaphors to describe death and dying, they are all misdirected. One does not 'follow'—one is not going anywhere. She didn't 'go' anywhere. Death is not a journey nor a destination; the dead are not travellers. We try to console ourselves with these metaphors—lies. They all harp on some sort of continuance. Alas, alas. [MS-3619/042]

In an undated typescript page tucked inside the same notebook, he reflects:

> She has gone, she will not come back. There is nothing of her to come back: nowhere is any space occupied by that which is or was her. She has gone, and she has taken with her the past as well as the future? What was the past, if not the permanent possibility of reviving shared experience? Without that possibility there is no past. As for memories, they are negations: their existence lies precisely

in the very absence, in the unrepeatability, of what is remembered. And they are nails of pain.

And yet she existed. How could destruction be so complete?

How we would twine about each other, wind our ways into each other, explore every physical and mental aperture in the desire to be two in one. We withheld nothing, nothing at all: you could hardly imagine. Or think rather of all possible forms of physical and mental giving: we found them all, and gave, wishing to reverse all repugnance and all privacy. How well we succeeded, you may see from my state now: I carried her inside me as the needle carries the earth's magnetism, and she has taken with her what was inside me so that, in an exact sense, I am dying for her who herself had no time to die. [MS-3619/042]

This was the insurmountable denial in Lonie's life; that love so hard won should be so brutally removed. Yet in 1986, during the fledgling period of his friendship with Ann Somerville, Lonie wrote: 'I wouldn't describe Judith's death as a shadow, though it has left me with a sadness: sometimes indeed it seems to be more like a blinding light of revelation; an ability from now on to see something about life and ourselves that most people don't see' [AS].

The proofs and related correspondence between Iain Lonie, Alan Loney (Voice Press) and Don McKenzie (Wai-te-ata Press) are in MS-3619/009 and MS-3619/017.

VII ⁓ The Classic Cast of Grief

The section title and epigraph come from a piece of card that is marked 'Poems 1983–1984' but also includes material collected in TETP and posthumously in WWAM [MS-2674/185]. The quotation 'che t'amo tanto / ch'usci per te della volgare schiera?' ('why have you not helped him who loves you so / that—for your sake—he's left the vulgar crowd?', trans. Allen Mandelbaum) is from Dante's *Inferno*, II:104–05; Paola Voci explains: 'The original verse is addressed to Beatrice from Lucia and she asks Beatrice to help the man (Dante) "who loved you".'

In his diary (December 1982 to March 1983) Lonie looked over his shoulder: 'Rhetoric—the rhetoric of grief. My own rhetoric in letters to friends, when I read it over, makes me cry—agreeably. What has it all to do with annihilation?' [MS-3619/042].

PURAKANUI BIRDCALL

Originally included in the computer printout of TETP dated 10 April 1985 [MS-2674/187]. On 19 June 1985 Bill Sewell, in a letter on behalf of John McIndoe accepting the collection *The Entrance to Purgatory*, suggested that this (and several other poems in the submitted typescript) be dropped. He described it as 'both hackneyed and pretentious: it's the sort of thing Cilla McQueen can get away with, but not you!' [MS-2674/189]. The official spelling of the place has subsequently been changed to Pūrākaunui (see also 'A Summer at Purakanui' in WWAM); however, I have preserved Lonie's spelling as accurate at the time of composition.

DEATH PORNO

Bill Sewell (see above) wrote: 'I'm not sure what you are trying to achieve ... but to me it doesn't ring true, although it might well do so in the hands of a lesser poet: the voice seems inauthentic' [MS-2674/189].

An entry in Lonie's diary (December 1982 to March 1983) shows how closely this poem circles the physical Judith Lonie:

> Today I am mostly conscious that I have lost my sexual playmate. No-one could wear stockings like her. How she epitomised for me all those film-stars of the forties, who haunted the dreams of my adolescence! You think this aspect of love a small one? How well she made my needs her own! You think this grief childish? Yes, it is childish: how children can grieve! [MS-3619/042]

'AND IN THAT WAY'

Perhaps worried by the echo of an early favourite, John Donne's *Holy Sonnets*, Lonie crossed out the final line of section 4 [MS-2674/187]; however, I have defied his ghost by restoring it here.

BRICOLAGE

Section 6 adopts the late version from AS, where Lonie has written corrections on a typescript sheet. He opens a notebook of drafts entitled 'Bricoleur' with: 'The poems are about junk, and as rough / but set it all down, *bricoleur*.' The notebook's cover bears the following epigraph from Canzone II of Dante's *Vita Nuova*: 'Che fai? non sai novella? / Morta e la donna tua, ch'era si bella' ('Come on. Do you know what befell? Your lady's dead, who was so beautiful', trans. Andrew Frisardi) [MS-4150/001].

In a letter dated 20 December 1984 Lonie resubmits the sequence to Hugh Lauder, then poetry editor of *Landfall*, after the journal had rejected it. He asserts:

> I have been writing for more years than I care to remember, and publishing in respectable periodicals, including *Landfall*, since 1952. In the last thirty-odd years my output, although not voluminous, has been consistent. I am not an eccentric, and I am an experienced enough poet to know when my own writing is bad and incompetent, and when it is not. Such a decision is part of the normal process of revision, rewriting and eventual rejection or submission to an editor, as it must be for any writer. I have made this decision about the set of poems in question, 'Bricolage'. I am just as aware of what I have tried to do in them, what methods I have used, as would be, say, a composer of music who had decided upon experiment in a particular mode. In such a case one might well not like the result, and one might not even be interested in it, which is a different matter again, but this would not be a sufficient reason for refusing the composer access to that critical public which is always larger than his personal acquaintance, or for refusing that public access to the work of the composer. The poems in question are the result of a great deal of direct work, and a great deal of experience and the judgement which goes with it. They are relatively complex, and need to be read carefully as a set. I am aware of their particular defects, but also, I think,

of their particular merits. I do not think they could be called either uninteresting or incompetent. If I am right in this opinion, then I think that given the unique position of *Landfall* in New Zealand, this is a sufficient reason for publishing them. [MS-3619/007]

On 8 March 1985 'Bricolage' was again rejected by Lauder: 'I appreciate the work you've put into these, the craft is apparent, but our opinion is that they don't really live. It may be that they've been overworked and have lost some spontaneity.' Lonie then appears to have abandoned attempts to publish the sequence.

Don McKenzie, writing to Bridie Lonie on 3 November 1988, revisited this pivotal exchange in partisan fashion:

> You'll probably remember the time when *Landfall* refused some of his poems: he was incensed, knew they were good, and that more fashionable notions had intruded to obscure and in effect suppress the far more enduring quality of his own work. But his poetry and its recognition, even by *Landfall*, were far too important to him to treat with dignified contempt this denial of what was, after all, a public formulation of the identity he'd striven so hard to define for himself and valued above all else. [MS-4150/004]

LIFELIKE

In a notebook entry dated 26 May 1985 Lonie confesses:

> Talking to John, Dave Brash's father in law, whose wife died a year ago. He said to me 'you'll still be feeling it,' and I made my usual reply about not seeing any reason why one should ever get over it.
> It has taken me a long time to realise it, but it doesn't matter what one says to anyone, no-one can enter into one's mind to share that particular bleakness. Not even those who must have felt something like it themselves. One is always going to be quite alone in grief, and the loneliness will never go. And if one goes on asking for a special conversation, particularly from the young, one is going to be disappointed and make a fool of oneself.
> In fact, most of us cope quite well in our outward behaviour, and that is all anyone will ever see of us, however much we want them to see more.
> If one could find someone to stand in the same bleak space as oneself, then by that very fact one would be cured. [MS-3619/044]

from 3½ POEMS ABOUT THE WEATHER FOR R.

'Autumn Thunder' from TETP was originally Part 3 of this sequence. See Section VIII and MS-2674/187.

THE FIRST OF MARCH

Appears to be the first page of 'But' in three folders [MS-2674/184, variant MS-2674/185, MS-2674/187]; however, a handwritten list of titles in the latter confirms they are discrete and places the poems on either side of 'The World Outside' [TETP].

'BUT'

Detail anticipates the posthumously published 'Proposal at Allans Beach' from WWAM (see Section X).

WAIKANAE, WITH VANESSA AND TOBY

A clean computer printout of the final text bears the authorial note: 'Vanessa is 12. Toby is 10. Toby is very interested in money and is going to make a lot of it when he grows up. Vanessa thinks she might like to be a concert pianist, and very famous. She thinks that she is grown up already' [MS-4150/008].

The children's father, Bill Manhire, wrote to Bridie Lonie on 15 August 1988: 'Anyway, I'm thinking about Iain at the moment ... we've just been out to Waikanae, where we last saw him: he and Andrew [Lonie's youngest son] pitched their tent in the garden, and then motored off for points north' [MS-4150/006].

A letter to Lonie dated 12 August 1988 (nearly two months after his death) from Lynne Loates of *More Magazine* returns poem and note, along with the contemporary pieces 'Distances', 'From the Heartland', and 'Unattended Crossing Ahead' [MS-4150/006].

VIII ∾ The Entrance to Purgatory (1986)

The original contents are in a computer printout dated 10 April 1985; an appendix dated 28 May 1985 contains 'The Compass Points North' [MS-2674/187]. On 2 June 1984 Bill Sewell, having been sent the poems, responded:

> I really don't know why you feel so dubious about those poems you asked me to read. They all show evidence of a steady hand; one is magnificent, and two or three others admirable. Is it because you fear they are too intensely personal? They are, but this in itself is nothing to shy away from, particularly as your poems are in no way heavy-handed. There is a calm and gentle irony which brings you a measure of detachment and makes them all the more moving … The poem I consider magnificent is 'The Entrance to Purgatory'. It is the kind of poem I aspire to write, flowing so beautifully and demonstrating a mastery of syntax so seldom found in New Zealand poets. I also appreciate its 'Classical' feel and the way it gives up its secrets only after repeated readings. The other poems I rate particularly highly are 'Theory of the Leisure Class, 1983', 'Ending the Sentence' and 'The World Outside'. [MS-2674/192]

On 18 February 1987 Kendrick Smithyman wrote to Lonie: 'I have been reading (and re-reading) *The Entrance to Purgatory*. May I say what fine poems they are, and how deeply moving?' [MS-3619/007].

VACUUM FLASK

Accepted by Andrew Mason for the *Listener* in a letter dated 20 February 1985 [MS-2674/187], its publication occasioned the following from Alan Roddick: 'A note to thank you for the poem in the *Listener*, "Vacuum Flask": a powerful moving poem whose last three lines had me in tears—"boring" was the word that struck me so forcefully—and I'm pleased that the *Listener* still has the good sense to print good poems such as yours, when so much of the magazine is frivolous and forgettable' [MS-2674/187].

In one of the few instances where poetry occasions love rather than the reverse, the publication led to Lonie's relationship with Ann Somerville. In a letter to this editor dated 21 May 2005 Ann remembered:

> The way we met is rather unusual. I was very taken with his poem 'Vacuum Flask' when it appeared in the *Listener*, and wrote to him via the editor. I received a note and a copy of *Courting Death*, and it carried on from there. He and Andrew [Lonie's youngest son] drove all the way up from Dunedin to meet me. The poem 'I want to remember it now' ['Journey North'] was written about that journey.

AUTUMN THUNDER

Originally Part 3 of the uncollected '3½ Poems About the Weather for R.'. The pieces 'I'm glad you rang' (1), 'I like you a lot' (2) and 'Can we meet again sometime?' (the '½' after 3) were also part of this sequence. See Section VII and MS-2674/187.

OLD FRIENDS

In 1986 Lonie explained to Ann Somerville:

> 'Old Friends' is really quite straightforward. It's a Louis MacNeice sort of poem, strong rhythms and repeated words or phrases rather than rhymes. It's meant to go with a swing, and in fact the repeated words ('went … all went', 'blueness … greyness', 'year … year', 'side … side' etc need to be given their full value to make it swing. The meaning is, stanza by stanza, 1. She left him by dying 2. for a time there was nothing but blank misery, fruitless memory of things left undone and unsaid 3. life comes back in the form of detail, obligations, the need to shop, answer letters, keep appointments ('surprising' because you'd think, after such grief, you could never bother about trivialities again) 4. and this is a mercy because it gets us going again, therefore these tiresome obligations are like old friends who help us away from the scene of an accident or a graveside perhaps, but also like old friends who carry us away drunk from a party we don't want to leave, so we're not grateful at being forcibly removed from our beloved grief. I suppose 'They were old friends' is

ambiguous: 'they' refers to the things which come back, fuss etc, not the he and she of the first line. I now realise that the title, followed immediately by 'He and she' is seriously misleading. But I'm quite pleased by this poem. [AS]

CRUSOE'S CANOE

The dedication to Elizabeth Smither was reciprocated; she dedicated 'In the Confessional' 'to Iain' and 'The Pet Cemetery' 'to Ia[i]n and Judith'; A3 photocopies of both are in the back of MS-2674/185.

IX ∾ The Heart's Hard Edge

A LATE HONEYMOON

Section 1, 'Voiles' (originally entitled 'Finite Hearts') and Section 2, 'Nuages', were published separately as 'A Late Honeymoon' and 'Nuages' in the posthumous WWAM. They are now restored to the original sequence. A printout [MS-4150/006] from Lonie's word processor, corrected in his hand, preserves the sequence but cancels the collective title 'Three Sea Images' in favour of 'A Late Honeymoon'. 'Voiles' has the cancelled subtitle 'a painting', while 'Nuages' has the cancelled subtitle 'Harriet Martineau at Tynemouth'.

JOURNEY NORTH

Composed during a road trip from Dunedin to Rotorua. For the circumstances, refer to the note on 'Vacuum Flask'.

372   *A Place To Go On From*

X ∽ Winter Walk at Morning (1991)

This posthumous volume drew upon a folder that Lonie marked 'Winter Walk—Originals Fair copy' [MS-4150/006]. This was used by Don McKenzie and Bill Manhire as they prepared the volume for publication by Victoria University Press. Their editorial decisions were also informed by manuscript and typescript versions [MS-4150/005 and MS-4150/007].

In a few instances apparently later versions, where the typescript is corrected by Lonie's hand, have been adopted from AS. Two pieces ('A Late Honeymoon' and 'Nuages') have been restored to the sequence 'A Late Honeymoon' (see Section IX) and therefore no longer appear here. Another, 'Hanging the Washing Out', tightens phrasing and adds a line to the previously published version.

The existence of multiple versions with many variant readings remains a vexed one for any editor. Rarely can there be certainty, although on 17 January 1991 McKenzie wrote to the publisher Fergus Barrowman: 'I feel fairly confident about the choice of text where there was more than one version of a poem' [MS-4150/006]. The same day he also wrote to Bridie Lonie: 'When I worked over the versions in detail the main problems in choice of readings seemed to disappear' [MS-4150/006].

HOLY LOCH

In a letter dated 14 April 1987, Bill Sewell comments on a draft:

> I do, I'm afraid, have some reservations about 'Holy Loch', even though I can appreciate the 'harpooned whales around the skirts / of a grey mother ship', the 'flotilla of geese' which hoots in Gaelic, and memory 'hoarding obsessively' for winter. But I worry that you are going over old territory in this poem, and wonder whether it constitutes any advance on 'Loch Ewe', for instance; and your play with the word 'mist' does not quite avoid the faithful old phrase 'mists of time' in 'objects / sunk in mists or layers of time'. If you are intending to be ironic, it is not made pointed enough. [MS-4150/007]

CALIBAN AT THE TYPEWRITER

In a letter to Ann Somerville dated Saturday 14 December (?1986) Lonie confirms:

> Caliban does as a matter of fact dance: he finds it profoundly satisfying in a way he can't account for, but which seems to let the emotions, the bad ones as well as the good, flow out through the fingers and the toes. And, of course, it's a splendid way of showing off. It's something I've only taken up again in the last year, having forgotten everything, and I'm still not good at it. [AS]

THE ART OF POETRY

In the typescript from 1987 this was originally headed 'Poetics: for Doug and Islay'. Lonie crossed this out, inserting the new title and dedication.

MIND YOUR HEAD

Completed four days before his suicide, this is Lonie's last poem. It closes the circle opened over thirty years earlier by Lonie's diary entry of 3 September 1950:

> I feel that insanity is very near. Give me strength to fight it off. I still know what it is to be healthy and happy and beautiful. I can still love. And I must not tell Jean [Lonie's first wife] about the struggle. As long as she trusts me, believes in my strength, then I shall trust and believe in myself. And I'm not insane yet. [MS-2674/105]

Writing to Bridie Lonie on 3 November 1988, Don McKenzie recalled: 'Iain had been half in love with death ever since we were boys in Palmerston North. I still vividly recall our conversation about hanging ourselves publicly from the Fitzherbert Bridge over the Manawatu River there when we were only 14 or 15' [MS-4150/004].

HANGING THE WASHING OUT

The version reproduced here, from AS, introduces minor if significant changes in phrasing and, crucially, a new line: 'a mote in the mind's eye' was pencilled in by Lonie to intensify the assonance of the mournful long O in neighbouring lines.

An early draft in MS-4150/004 was originally entitled 'A Letter'; Lonie cancelled this and substituted 'Apology for Hanging Out the Washing'.

MS-4150/006 contains a clean typescript of the earlier version used in WWAM, now entitled 'Hanging the Washing Out', alongside a letter dated 24 January 1991 from publisher Fergus Barrowman to Bridie Lonie: 'I understand you and Don [McKenzie] have had some discussion about the inclusion or not of "Hanging Out the Washing". Bill Manhire and I talked about it this morning; we think it's a very strong and moving poem, and are keen to see it in.'

XI ~ Being Outside Time: versions from Eugenio Montale (1985–87)

In a letter to Lonie dated 14 April 1987, Bill Sewell writes:

> I'm writing because I've had your Montale translations and poem 'Holy Loch' sitting in my office for over a month now, and I realise I haven't given you any response to them. The reason is not that I've been impossibly busy, or that they displease me (and I'm reluctant to say). It's simply that I find the Montale pieces either enigmatic ('Within/Without'), or disarmingly banal ('Jovian'). The exception is 'Letter from the Riviera di Levante', which I have seen before, and which has a narrative component and a rhetoric that I can easily respond to. One thing I will say though: they all read extremely well, with a mixture of the colloquial and the formal, which you manage so well. And though these are translations, the dry, philosophical tone is entirely natural to you. On the whole, though, there is more 'colour' in your own poems. [MS-4150/007]

The tonal appeal of Montale for Lonie's own poetry is shown by the difficulty of identification. Reading the working drafts one wonders: 'Whose is this?' Don McKenzie, writing to the publisher Fergus Barrowman about *Winter Walk at Morning*, observed:

> I don't *think* I have included any which might be thought to be translations of Montale poems. The Harriet Martineau one gave me pause, and others have overtones. But I checked out the collection with a colleague in Oxford (his doctorate was on Pasolini as a lyric poet but he's also well up on Montale). His verdict was that the collection itself has no Montale translations in it. [17 January 1991, MS-4150/006]

LETTER FROM THE RIVIERA DI LEVANTE

In an undated letter, probably from 1986, Lonie wrote to Ann Somerville:

> This poem by Montale is better than any letter by me could be, and in fact I thought quite a lot about us when I was translating it. Some of it you may find almost uncanny—I hope so. Don't know anything about the background. It was written in 1924, but apparently not published till after his death, in 1980. The Riviera di Levante is on the NW of Italy, just where it runs around to join France. The Alps there (I believe—I've never seen it) come right down to the coast—it must look a bit like the Kaikoura Coast (which I hope we'll see together in January). The Cinqueterre, or 'Five countries', is apparently another name for that region. I can't tell you any more. [AS]

In fact the original was written in 1923, when Montale was 27, as Lonie notes on the corrected typescript in MS-4150/006; it is collected in *Alti Versi* (Mondadori, 1981), which Lonie owned no later than June 1986.

'SINCE LIFE ESCAPES US'

This version from Montale's late collection *New Poems* was typed, corrected, yet left unfinished. Lonie cancelled 'labyrinth' (line 3) and 'verbal wit' (line 10), marking the latter 'ambiguous'—yet he offered no replacements. The source poem echoes a statement by Montale in 1946:

> Besides, poetry is only one of a great many positives in life. I don't think a poet is more significant than anyone else who truly exists, who is someone. I too acquired a smattering of psychoanalysis in its time, but even without its lights I thought early, and still think, that art is the form of life of a man who doesn't really live: a compensation or surrogate. Which is not to justify a deliberate ivory-tower attitude. A poet must not renounce life; it is life that tries to flee from him.

This quote appears in a review of Montale's *New Poems* and *Pequod* that was published in *The American Poetry Review* (November/December 1978), a photocopy of which is clipped to Lonie's version [MS-4150/003].

'GOOD LINUCCIA, YOU WHO CLIMB'

A version of 'Buona Linuccia che ascendi', *Altri Versi* (Mondadori, 1981, p. 130). Lonie's copy of the Italian first edition is inscribed 'Iain Lonie/ June 1986'; however, his manuscript draft is on the back of an Otago Catchment Board document dated 8 February 1985. Lonie recycled multiple copies of this official document (see also the note to 'A Visitor'). The version here is from the corrected typescript [MS-4150/003].

MY FRIEND PÉA

Line 3: 'and telephoned room service to send up lunch'—Lonie notes: 'Lit: "ordered the waiter to serve lunch". I don't know why I indulged this flight of fancy.'

Line 8: 'pity for everything, for man, a little perhaps for himself'—Lonie notes: 'Lit: "a bit less for himself"' [MS-4150/003].

OBOE

Lines 6–7: 'because they haven't made the headlines, because / nobody knows they are eyes and ears'—Lonie notes: 'a mistake. Galassi: "because down here / no newspapers arrive, and no-one knows / that there are eyes and ears"' [MS-4150/003]. *Otherwise: Last and First Poems of Eugenio Montale*, trans. Jonathan Galassi (Vintage, 1984).

MONOLOGUE

Lines 13–14: 'of something we hadn't quite reached / when the time came to break off'—Lonie notes: 'a ludicrous mistake: "where something / that hasn't reached the breaking point is bubbling", Galassi' [MS-4150/003].

'HOW THE HORIZON NARROWS'

Lonie notes: '"existlessness" is used, with great poignancy, by Hardy. The "ant" I suspect is an allusion to Montale's dead wife, whom he sometimes calls "mosca" or fly' [MS-4150/003].

HIDING PLACES

Line 3: 'but only spray ever entered that specimen'—Lonie notes: 'specimen, prova. Galassi translates "rehearsal"' [MS-4150/003].

A VISITOR

Line 14: 'I haven't seen her since: today I suppose'—Lonie notes: 'a mistake: "I never saw her"' [MS-4150/003].

Along with 'Succulents', a typescript is printed on the reverse of a form letter, dated 8 February 1985, from the Otago Catchment Board [MS-4150/003]. This recycled paper stock was also used for 'Good Linuccia, You Who Climb'.

'MY SWISS WATCH WAS FAULTY'

Line 6: 'this distancing oneself from an appointment'—Lonie quotes the original Italian and notes: 'a mistake: "this prolonging of the appointment"' [MS-4150/003].

'TO ME IT'S JUST IMPOSSIBLE'

Lines 7–8: 'body of the incorporeal could outweigh / the heaven you fill'—Lonie notes: 'literally, "not even the incorporeal / can equal your heaven"' [MS-4150/003].

A PUPIL OF THE MUSES

Line 1: 'Pack your suitcase, my child'—Lonie notes: '"satchel" Galassi'.
    Line 10: 'of the Gods is different from ours'—Lonie notes: 'sarà: *will be* different' [MS-4150/003].

'WIPE YOUR GLASSES IF THEY ARE DIMMED'

Line 9: 'upon some more terrifying happiness'—Lonie notes: 'literally "putting at our disposal the access to some more terrifying happiness"' [MS-4150/003].

So Iain Lonie closes his account as a translator. Thirty years earlier he told Charles Brasch, 'I find I can learn nothing from translations—or, indeed, poetry in another language' (see the note to 'The Achaeans'). But Lonie would turn to the Italians Dante and Montale; they calibrated the influence of his contemporary Peter Porter, a lesser Auden, ensuring that Lonie rose to the challenge issued in Montale's 1931 essay 'On Contemporary Poetry', rendered here by Lonie's guide Jonathan Galassi:

> The poet must not only give vent to his own emotion, he must also work his own verbal material "into a certain sign," he must provide what Eliot calls "an objective correlative" for his own perception. Only when it reaches this level does poetry come into existence and leave an echo of, an obsession with, itself. Sometimes it lives on its own and the poet doesn't recognise it any more: it doesn't matter. [*The Second Life of Art: Selected Essays of Eugenio Montale* (Ecco Press, 1982), p. 290]

David Howard

Index of titles

11.30 from Liverpool Street 288
3½ Poems About the Weather for R. 212

Academic Architecture 147
Achaeans, The 76
Afternoon Tea in the East 157
Allardyce 59
Among the Ruins 248
Ancestral Ground 292
Anomalous Behaviour 183
April the First 308
Art of Poetry, The 309
At Least 282
At Pearl Bay 96
Autumn Thunder 236

Blankness of Snow, The 219
Bricolage 206
Brouillards 266
By a River 63
By Definition 279
By Foreign Hands 184

Caliban at the Typewriter 297
Cambridge in the Fifties 288
Can we meet again sometime? 214
Cardboard Box 206
Change of Season on the Way to the Station 164
Choices 228
Coastguard's House, The 343
Collection Day 318

Compass Points North, The 258
Conversation 217
Cosi vidi venir, traendo guai, ombre portate dalla detta briga 87
Country Hard to Imagine, A 252
Country Walk with Guide-book 163
Cranach: Adam and Eve 209
Creatures of the Fire 186
Crusoe's Canoe 241
Cunning Odysseus 97
Cupboard Love 192
Cut Glass I 207
Cut Glass II 208

Daybreak 342
Dead Letter 227
Dead Reckoning 286
Death 110
Death of a Culture 166
Death Porno 201
Dee Why Morning 134
Dialogue 81
Dispossession: staccato 237
Distances 303
Divide, The 198
Dolce Vita 209
Dual Number 205
Dull Man, Essentially, A 172
Dunedin Weather 139

Electra 109
Elegy to Maecenas 90

Elegy, Armidale Cemetery 78
Ending the Sentence 240
Entrance to Purgatory, The 260
Epitaph 135
Erinna's Lament for Baukis 135
Evening 60
Exile 291

Fine Definitions 247
First of March, The 215
Five o'clock 185
Flat in WC1, A 246
Flying Back 225
Flying Back 226
Folk Memory 294
Forced Listener, The 84
Four Sydney Photographs 145
Fragment 59
Friends at the Funeral 176
Frog Prince, The 230
From a Point of View 94
From Academy Hill 143
From the Heartland 313

Ghosts 186
Glacier 125
Grand Meaulnes, Le 277
Green Bird, The 131
Green Bottle 206

Hanging the Washing Out 321
Harriet Martineau: First
   Intimations of Politics and
   Death 315
Haunted House 220
Hay Field, The 67
Her Dreams 87
Her Room 86
Here is My Song for Death:
   Lydian Chant 214
Hiding Places 336

Holiday Notes 60
Holy Loch 304
Home Thoughts from
   Abroad 169
Homoeoteleuton 178
Horace's Girlfriends 245
House of Childhood, The 220

I like you a lot 213
Ibycus 153
Idiot's Song 71
I'm glad you rang 212
Im wunderschönen Monat
   Mai 234
In Padua 248
In the Mill Lane Lecture Rooms 289
In the Third Person 253
Interviews of Eyes 199

Jazz Record Requests 173
Journey North 269
Jovian 332

Kallimachos of Kyrene 91
Knowing the Right Places 309

Last Night 88
Late Honeymoon, A 265
Letter from a Distance 65
Letter from a Ferry 69
Letter from Ephesus 148
Letter from the Riviera di
   Levante 327
Letter in December 279
Lifelike 200
Lifer 74
Lines on a Photograph 211
Lines on a Photograph 290
Loch Ewe 250

Matutinal 95
Memories of Ithaca 160

Index of titles

Mind Your Head 321
Mirror Language 295
Monologue 334
Morning 60
Morning Calm 68
My Friend Péa 333
My Toaster Tells the Time 307

Nearly So 301
Night Garden, with Ghost 234
Night Passage 60
Not a Poem 276
Nothing to Do with Us 139
Now We Are 168
Nuages 266

Oblique View, An 255
Oboe 334
Ode to Walter 158
Odysseus in Travelland 285
Old Friends 239
On the Equator 194
Orpheus to Eurydice 104

Philemon and Baucis 286
Pieces of Occasion 225
Pioneers 170
Point of No Return 184
Possession: legato 238
Postcard of Cornwall, A 193
Proposal at Allans Beach 319
Pupil of the Muses, A 341
Purakanui Birdcall 197

Real McCoy, The 73
Reflets dans l'eau 281
Remarks on a Landscape
   Painting 73
Request for a Birthday Poem 92
Rome 1965 225

Saying and Meaning 177

Scottish Mill Towns 64
Sea Fog, The 66
Second Chance 210
Short Story 127
Slow Glass 268
Solstice 58
Song 62
Sonnet 63
Street Scene 144
Studies 152
Succulents 338
Summer at Purakanui, A 296
Summer Night, A 174
Sydney 251

Talent 205
Tarawera 61
Tarawera, Lake & Mountain 269
Territorial Dispute 168
Theory of the Leisure Class,
   1983 246
Things No Longer Simple 210
Third Party 177
Tonight 192
Traditio 125
Travel Diary 193
Truth 199
Two Houses 140
Two Nocturnes 237
Two Predicates 306

Ugolino and His Sons 137
Unattended Crossing Ahead 314

Vacuum Flask 230
Val di Chiana 250
Variation on an Old Theme 316
Visit 231
Visitor, A 337
Voices 267
Voiles 265

Waikanae, with Vanessa and Toby 221
Waking Up in Naples 299
Watching War Films 278
We Are All in a Painting 244
West Berlin: Unorchestrated Notes 158
'Whitley Rocks' 175
'Why, When I Speak, Do You Never Answer?' 183
Wickliffe Bay 66
Wind at Rimini, The 86
Winter Strawberries 176
Winter Walk at Morning, The 311
Witch 75
Within/Without 339
World Outside, The 232
Wrack 208

Your Dream 231
Your Old Age 229
Your Story 173

Index of first lines

A beautiful dark haired girl runs 171
A canteen is provided 165
A distant relative of mine was a collector 338
A frost last night 282
a gesture engraved upon air 173
A slight accident 229
Actually I find it much easier 297
Adjectives—something thrown in for good measure 93
After the dark had come, the wind dropped suddenly 66
After the evening calm, the wind 250
After the storm is past, I hear the sea 68
After years, he learned to welcome the summer 114
Ah, little use, now that I'm bleeding 62
All that night, and through the next and through the next 107
All the starlings on all the telephone wires in the world 212
Already we are strange 139
and in that way 202
And then again, this endless need I have 206
And was it here, six months ago 63
Another person, say, is a context: an attitude 94
As the grey river brought me round again 84
At the class in navigation we were warned 286
At the last moment, your eyes 199
At whoring I was ineffectual 65

Basalt capes 319
Battered by rains through July, August, September 168
Between the time of you and I 105
Bowing your head, you kneel 244
But 216
By rust of weapon 59

Clouds do not move 266

Coming down the stairs 240
Coming down upon Stockton from the North York moors 209
Contractors are demolishing 144
Cunning Odysseus, cunning Penelope 97

Dear Ann, this present I enclose 275
Dear Bridie: entering upon 92
Deferring to our greying tutors (younger 289
Do not go too near 125
Do not misunderstand me: I too comprehend 166
Do you remember 250
Don't imagine that two people 236

Each morning the cat backs up 309
east 313
Encased in our winged time machine 226
Even to see is hard enough 131

For journeys into the past, you must 316
From plain to mountain air, from Trasimene up 253

Give to all youth this I have known 64
God alone knows all my mind 71
Good Linuccia, you who climb 332
Good spot for a picnic 301
Grace in this landscape is hard to find. If you rise 116
Gradually we deplete the larder 192
Grief is stronger than fear 183

Half an hour, by the arterial 145
Having taken that decision, you could not see 83
He stayed, and she went 239
Here is my song for death 214
Here is the painting that you chose 228
Hills were always elsewhere, lost 255
His patron provided them, with so much else 245
How archaic now the clipped syllables 173
How are the shops in Hades—are they good? 104
How many will read these words 306
How the horizon narrows 335

I am a country, she says—here are my mountains 87
I am a small boy 171

Index of first lines

I am watching you write a poem 201
I do not claim 121
I don't like the poems that everyone reads, the load 91
I drove past your house last night 89
I had invited you to my private feast 125
I have discovered this marvellous poet 211
I have not had the heart 318
I haven't yet written you a love poem 276
I pause before each of you, folding your hands together 176
I should like these syllables 327
I smoke, drink, read, watch the sky 60
I tell you, there is a great bog in this country 169
I unpack such things from memory, and wonder 206
I want to remember, now 269
I watched you walk along that mile of beach 220
If in the morning 124
If you could tell the dawn was coming 88
If you should enter now 199
Impulsive, as ever 177
In Billings' timber 134
In Ephesus they believe in change 148
In Macquarie Street 146
In the dim light of the smoking compartment 288
In the end, they bring what one wants, the lean obsequious years 90
In the flat opposite 308
In the old days there would have been banquets to propitiate 69
In the spring and autumn, mice invade my house 114
In this photograph 153
In washing dishes, she sought her usual end 167
Inter- 158
Is to take one last cool look around the room 110
It is not all unpleasant, waiting for 238
It is the first day of winter now 67
It may happen at any time, for any cause: your pen 101
It was as if they were dreaming 281
It was too early for such a visit 231
It's long since I gazed 334
I've just hung the print I discovered 279
I've set the programme: water trickles down like rain 321

Kostas and I sat 127

Laughing, we landed and lugged the boat 60
Leaves fall, leaves fall 112
Lift your head, stag, lift your antlered head 113
Like a stroke of lightning 213
Long after the sun had gone 267
Look, said she, who can remember all things 75
Look, we can make miracles 269

Mad girl, from the white horse's back 135
Mind your head, you said, as I walked down the stair 321
My dreams are slow to learn 230
My grief's a black hole where my father lies 109
My grin a rictus splitting from ear to ear 137
My love 170
My Swiss watch was faulty 340

No doubt the architect was pulling our legs 147
No fog: merely a thickening of air 93
Not able to live with the here and now, my mind's 208
Not one of these poems is good 205
Not the breath of the rabble, acrid with lust now 108
Now he has gone, in petulance or boredom 104
Now one has gone from me, and coming night 63
Now spring dawns in our months of passion 57

O where are you now, my Hebrides 59
On earth 332
On my desk 152
On the sand hill, lupin blooms 102
Once again I recognise that coast black as iron 82
One may grow angry with it: it is like a person 106
One should not revisit an old house. I don't care 140
One side: time 307
Oranges were ripening all along the tracks 299
Out there on the still 304
Out there where the spilled city began 311

Pack your suitcase, my child 341
Passing the grey stone farmhouse 220
Peace and quiet may be sought 73

Index of first lines

Perhaps it is its death that fascinates 80
Pines glide their green glacier down 61
Poems presenting themselves as summons: a cold grip 258
Pythagoras, all hail 158

rain comes again, and wind to sweep the rain 192
Rubbing my hand along the rough-cast wall 57

She is young, young as the green grape 113
She lies sleeping now 172
Shop windows turn their light upon the street 101
Since life escapes us 331
Since we two happened together 60
So warm last night, we lay 139
Some men have never had the fire 73
Some poems have no plan 314
Some women, they say, in your circumstances 103
Something in us too is ground 296
Sometimes the Demiurge (God's fall-guy 334
Spring: Ky- 153
St Peter: Have you ever done … 81
Still ignorant of his power, he essayed 107
Sunday afternoon. The week hung wavering 58

That reed bed where I used to go and hide 336
That spring when we read 277
That was how it was, it was just like that 200
The air will do something to our skin: burn it 291
The barley, rumpled 163
The blue air of a Sunday afternoon 143
The blue-grey canister 278
The children across the road were undesirable 115
The City Hospital 152
The dress you wear 103
The evenings are hot. Hotter, I think, as the summer advances 218
The ferry rail 251
The fisherman's line startled 58
The fungus in the sky is still no bigger 246
The Greeks had a word for it 279
The harbour wall, sunlight on the water 193
The memory of your voice is fading 194

The name attracted us 309
The new insurance building, providential 146
The notion of death came to me early 315
The pathway on this headland 178
The pilgrims on their way to consult Apollo 252
The pines aren't Respighi's 225
The portly singer clings with one hand to the piano 234
The Qantas pilot, pivoting 146
The river is flowing backwards 268
The rose-tree in my garden grew suddenly still 75
The sea 221
The sea was calm that day, the sky clear 96
The snow looming at night through frosted glass 219
The snow melts quickly from the hills 121
The sun's fireball, suddenly released 95
The things one buys on holidays 247
The tree of life may grow outside your cell 74
The trees swept scarlet to the water's edge 285
The two of you 205
The Wall opens for us 157
The weather advances 214
The wind gets up tonight 215
The wind (there's always wind 290
The wine, the wine 160
The worst part is the waking dream. Earlier 111
The writer imagines not 342
The years that were wasted, the years 266
Their forefathers, moving through a fluent 76
Their forefathers, moving through a fluent 110
Their names uncouth on the tongue as flint 64
There is something 217
There is this dialogue 183
There were winter strawberries in the market today 176
These places that seem half factory, half—what 292
These spring nights, you want to take off 234
They lie so quiet 78
They lived with great contentment in an ad 286
Things that are no longer simple 210
Thinking of you—but have you not said enough 84
This is the hour 185

This is your dream: me 231
This man perished beyond the speed of sound 108
This music takes me back five years 174
This was the last 232
Though your things in this room are there to appease the eye 86
To chop up vegetables into chunks, slash through 246
To hide one's madness among the mad 111
To me it's just impossible 340
To this uncentred self the world of strangers 225
To you, my dear, my thoughts go from this bed 65
Towards the dawn, slow Orion turned 77

Unaccompanied by dog or memory 133

Waiting for sleep at night 237
Warbler 197
We are wearing exactly the clothes 265
We can't go on meeting like this 295
We got out when the train stopped 248
We pedal abreast, amicably wrangling 303
We return from a walk together: the blood jabs 129
We took flight at last 184
We took the inland route, against 198
We who never cared for gardens 117
Weathereye 135
What did it remind me of, that wind? 164
What you will notice first is the air's 260
When Leopoldo Fregoli heard death's tread 333
When Morgan 154
When reality becomes disjointed 339
When the act we would 105
When you were seven you made a parachute 168
Whenever our aunt from Pietrasanta 337
Why do you put up with me? 122
Why will you stand so, against the winter sky 62
Wind came that day, darkening the sea's blue 87
Wipe your glasses if they are dimmed 341
With *Everyman his owne Shipwright* in one hand 241

You cannot look upon me here 186
You deal kindly with me today: sliding 209

You died at nineteen. You never married   132
You don't remember the coastguard's house   343
You follow behind   186
You have left your book   230
You lay in a blue chapel   184
You, once in your life, became able   210
You planted cemeteries on slopes   294
You told me of this poet once   177
You will not look   193
Your blue glass catches the moon—so far, so far   208
Your card came, over a year too late   227
Your mind is filled with dusty *bric a brac*   207
Your picture is glowing tonight   175
Your word sometimes seems   122